D1602361

POYLN
My Life within Jewish Life in Poland,
Sketches and Images

Poyln

My Life within Jewish Life in Poland, Sketches and Images

YEHIEL YESHAIA TRUNK

Translated from the Yiddish by Anna Clarke

Edited by Piotr Wróbel and Robert M. Shapiro

UNIVERSITY OF TORONTO PRESS
Toronto Buffalo London

Printed in Canada

ISBN 978-08020-9330-1

Printed on acid-free paper

Library and Archives Canada Cataloguing in Publication Data

Trunk, Yehiel Yeshaia, 1887–1961.
    Poyln : my life within Jewish life in Poland : sketches and images / Yehiel
    Yeshaia Trunk ; translated from the Yiddish by Anna Clarke ; edited by Piotr
    Wróbel and Robert M. Shapiro.

    ISBN 978-0-8020-9330-1

    1. Jews – Poland – History.   2. Jews – Poland – Social life and customs.
    3. Trunk, Yehiel Yeshaia, 1887–1961.   4. Trunk family.   5. Hasidism – Poland.
    6. Jews, Polish – Biography.   7. Authors, Yiddish – Biography.   I. Clarke,
    Anna   II. Wróbel, Piotr   III. Shapiro, Robert Moses   IV. Title.

    PJ5129.T77P6513 2007   839′.18309   C2007-902126-3

University of Toronto Press acknowledges the financial assistance to its
publishing program of the Canada Council for the Arts and the Ontario Arts
Council.

University of Toronto Press acknowledges the financial support for its
publishing activities of the Government of Canada through the Book
Publishing Industry Development Program (BPIDP).

Contents

vi Contents

Editor's Preface

Poyln, by Yehiel Yeshaia Trunk, initiates a new editorial series devoted to the history of Polish Jews. Published under the auspices of the Polish-Jewish Heritage Foundation of Canada, Toronto Chapter, and the Konstanty Reynert Chair of Polish History at the University of Toronto, the series aims at presenting all aspects of the rich history of Polish Jews and to reclaim their legacy, almost destroyed during the Holocaust and in danger of being forgotten in North America. The aim of the series can best be summarized in the words of Rabbi Byron L. Sherwin: 'Only when what existed in Poland before the Holocaust is understood can one truly discern the dimensions of the loss. From this perspective, it is important for Jews today to see Poland not only as a huge Jewish cemetery, but also as a country where Jews created unprecedented works of the spirit, as a land where Judaism flourished freely and developed beyond what previously had been, as a landscape dotted with Jewish spiritual monuments.'[1]

The present book is the first volume of *Poyln.* The main body of the text has been translated by Anna Clarke, who had previously translated excerpts from *Poyln* into both Polish and English. Piotr Wróbel wrote an introduction and prepared the footnotes, a family tree for Trunk, and a map of Trunk's Poland. Robert M. Shapiro, Assistant Professor of Judaic Studies at Brooklyn College

---

1 Byron L. Sherwin, *Sparks amidst the Ashes: The Spiritual Legacy of Polish Jewry* (New York and Oxford: Oxford University Press, 1997), 7.

of the City University of New York, translated Trunk's Prologue and reviewed the translation and the footnotes. *Poyln* is a moving testimony, a colourful epic, and an extremely interesting book. Until now, only small fragments of it have been translated into English. We are proud to present for the first time in English the entire first volume of *Poyln*.

Piotr Wróbel
Konstanty Reynert Chair of Polish History
University of Toronto

Introduction

Poyln (Poland) is one of the treasures of world literature. Written in early-twentieth-century Polish Yiddish, it has so far been unavailable in English. Its author, Yehiel Yeshaia Trunk, was an outstanding Polish Jewish writer, and *Poyln* is an important historical primary source.

Trunk was born in 1887 in the village of Osmólsk, not far from Warsaw, into a rich family of Jewish landowners on his mother's side and of scholars and rabbis on his father's side. After several years of carefree childhood in the village of Dłutów, he and his family moved to Łódź, a big industrial city in the centre of Russian-occupied Poland. There, Trunk received a traditional religious education, but at the same time he was taught secular subjects by private tutors who, among other things, gave their pupil a good knowledge of several languages.

Trunk started writing in Hebrew. His first texts were written in 1905, when, in a personal diary, he described revolutionary events in Łódź. Soon, however, he was to change his literary voice from Hebrew to Yiddish. Trunk's father, a successful entrepreneur, was an avid reader. He studied international literature and knew personally the great Jewish writer Isaac Leib Peretz (1852–1915). Under the influence of Peretz, Trunk switched to Yiddish and sought to achieve a synthesis of modern European and traditional Jewish literary and intellectual trends. Like Oyzer Warszawski (1898–1944), Alter Kacyzne (1885–1941), Moshe Justman (1889–1942), Israel Joshua Singer (1893–1944), and Isaac

Bashevis Singer (1905–91), Trunk adhered to Peretz's naturalist style. From 1908 on, he published fiction, poems, essays, and criticism, mostly in journals and books edited by Peretz. Trunk also wrote articles for newspapers, sometimes in Hebrew, on contemporary cultural, scholarly, and philosophical issues. Together with his wife, Khane Prywes, a granddaughter of the 'King of Iron,' Isaiah Prywes, Trunk travelled extensively in Europe, Africa, and Asia. In 1913–14 he spent twelve months in Palestine. Later he described his Palestinian observations in a volume entitled *Fig Trees* (*Faygnboymer*, 1922). The most outstanding achievement of his early period was a collection of tales, *Of Nature* (*Fun der natur*), published in 1914 in Warsaw. Beautifully illustrated by the famous Polish Jewish painter Artur Szyk (1894–1951), the book became an artistic event when it was launched.

During the First World War, Trunk lived in Switzerland. In 1919 he returned to Poland, whose independence had been restored, and settled in Łódź. He became a successful partner in an extensive textile enterprise and lived in a palatial house with a big garden, but in 1923 he joined the Bund, the largest Jewish social-democratic party in Poland. In the same year he published his critical study on Oscar Wilde's *Dorian Grey*. Trunk intensified his literary activities after 1925, when he moved to Poland's capital, Warsaw. There he served as president of the Jewish PEN Club and was one of the pillars of Jewish cultural life. He published more literary criticism, including two works on the writer Sholem Aleichem (1859–1916), and a number of novels and stories. Living on one of the most elegant streets of Warsaw and pursuing an aristocratic way of life, he still supported the Bund's social aspirations and Jewish Diaspora nationalism. In *Yiddishism and Jewish History* (1930), he developed the ideas of the great Jewish historian Simon Dubnow (1860–1941), who claimed that shared history and common language were more important than territory in keeping Jews together as a nation. Trunk defended Yiddishism and suggested that Hebrew should retain its role as the Latin of the Jews.

Before the Second World War, Trunk, aware of the threat posed by Hitler, was involved in anti-Fascist activities. Therefore, after the German invasion of Poland on 1 September 1939, the Bund leadership ordered the writer to escape. Trunk and his wife moved to Vilna, in eastern Poland, but that city was occupied by the Soviets later that month. (Although the Soviets almost immediately ceded Vilna to Lithuania, the Red Army reoccupied the city in the summer of 1940.) In Vilna, Trunk worked for YIVO, the Jewish Scientific Institute, but in 1940 he left the city and, through Siberia, Japan, and San Francisco, reached New York in March 1941. Before the war one of the richest Jews in Poland, he had not invested or deposited money abroad. He arrived in New York penniless, and for the rest of his life he had to struggle for daily bread. Yet this difficult period proved to be very fruitful. Trunk wrote several historical novels, works of literary criticism, and stories based on the Jewish folklore of Eastern Europe and depicted such characters as the fools of Chełm, the famous false Messiah Sabbatai Zvi, and the founder of Hasidism, the Ba'al Shem Tov.

Two days after he landed in New York, Trunk started writing his memoir, *Poyln*. He spent over ten years on this project, and in the years 1944–53, seven volumes were published. Already in 1941 Trunk knew that the Jews in Poland were facing a catastrophe of biblical proportions, and from his apartment in the Washington Heights area of Manhattan he followed the Holocaust of European Jewry.

Poyln is a family chronicle, an autobiography, a nostalgic epic portrait of Polish Jewry, and it is Trunk's response to the destruction of his people. The book is sometimes described as a portable literary gravestone for a destroyed community, a form of commemoration, or an attempt to recreate 'a world that is no more,' to use the title of I.J. Singer's autobiography (1946). Trunk's book resembles the works of Chaim Grade (1910–82), the Singer brothers, and also Marcel Proust's *In Search of Lost Time* (1913–27). *Poyln*'s hero is the national community of Polish Jews. To portray this community, the author describes a rich gallery of types of several branches of his family tree: Hasidic patricians, timber merchants, rich landowners, and affluent entrepreneurs; brilliant Talmudists, Orthodox rabbis, and Hasidic *tsadikim*. He also depicts ordinary village and small-town Jews, artisans, shop-keepers, workers, and *Luftmentshn,* all of them members of one extended family. Trunk puts them in different eras, places, and situations; he shows their habits and customs, their psychic features and beliefs; he discusses different trends in the Hasidic movement; he tries to build a bridge between his secular generation and its religious ancestors; and he shows himself as a product of the previous generations. In short: he shows Jewishness as a way of life.

Trunk is a storyteller, with a good dose of humour, irony, and even some caricature and grotesque elements. His style includes a good deal of stylization, nostalgia, and much warmth, dynamism, and satire. Trunk has empathy for the poor, and he laughs at the rich. A particular strength and perhaps uniqueness of the book is its rich gallery of Jewish women, rich and poor, sophisticated and uneducated, happy and miserable, good and bad. It would also be difficult to find another memoir in which the life of Polish village Jews and their difficult and diversified relationship with Christians was described in as much detail and colour.

Poyln proved to be very popular among Yiddish readers and was reprinted many times. Written in small feuilleton-like chapters with captions, like the cheap chapbooks and pamphlets sold once in the Jewish streets of Eastern Europe, the text is easy to follow and comprehend. Some literary critics frowned upon allegedly too many humorous and grotesque scenes and characters on the pages of *Poyln.* Trunk answered that if he had wanted to write objectively and at a distance, only a sea of tears would have come out. The book received the Louis Lamed Award from the National Foundation for Jewish Culture. Some critics believed that Trunk should be considered one of the most outstanding luminaries of Yiddish literature.

Piotr Wróbel

Legend
——— contemporary borders
—·—·— pre-1914 borders
— — — 1918–39 borders

Map of Poland: the most important towns and cities mentioned by Y.Y. Trunk

Family Tree

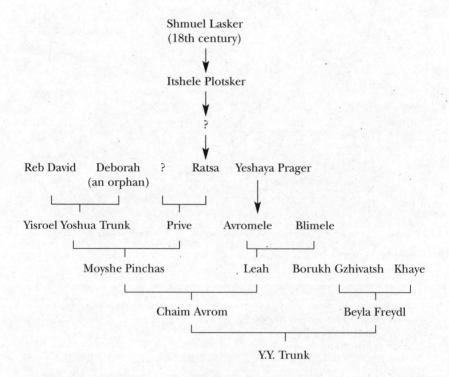

Shmuel Lasker
(18th century)
↓
Itshele Plotsker
↓
?
↓

Reb David   Deborah   ?   Ratsa   Yeshaya Prager
(an orphan)
                                        ↓

Yisroel Yoshua Trunk   Prive   Avromele   Blimele

Moyshe Pinchas   Leah   Borukh Gzhivatsh   Khaye

Chaim Avrom   Beyla Freydl

Y.Y. Trunk

POYLN
My Life within Jewish Life in Poland,
Sketches and Images

Prologue

The present book is the first of a series of volumes in which I want to present a portrait of my family within the framework and in relation to a portrait of Jewish life in Poland.

In Poland, Jewish life was deeply rooted in the soil and in the landscape, and from those juices flowed the whole Jewish creativity. The bitter and tragic fate of Jewish history arrived like a dark storm over the full and wonderful Jews of Poland, deep and whole Jews in their classes and in their stations. From those Jews floated the holy fragrance of living Jewish continuity. 'The fragrance of the fields that G-d has blessed.' The sword has been brought down on their heads, and in their spilled blood the enemy of the world wanted to see the end of the eternal Jewish nation.

But Polish Jews are not so easily removed from their settled places. The old Jewish heroism always shone from their traditions and from their revolutions, from their pieties and from their heresies. In Poland we had the privilege to see with our own eyes a portrait of the ancient Jewish people.

The last Jewish fighters in the ghetto are to be compared in their fashion to the fighters during the destruction of Jerusalem. The struggle of Jews in the Polish towns and shtetls, the struggle of Jews with the enemies of the world, is among the handsomest models of human exaltation. To the Jews in Poland, among whom are my father, Chaim Avrom, and my mother, Beyla Freydl, is this book dedicated.

Y. Y. Trunk
New York, 3 November 1943

The autobiography of a person does not necessarily start with the personal images of life that he drags out of his own recollections. Taken as a whole, the person is the sum total of preceding generations and their product. The person is no more than the synthesis of a long history. I want to begin my memoirs with the genealogy of my parents.

(Translated by Robert M. Shapiro)

Chapter One

Grandfather Borukh Gzhivatsh comes from a family of common Jews. Duke Sapieha. The meek and pious Grandmother Khaye. The only child is a gift in answer to prayers.

My maternal grandfather, Borukh Gzhivatsh, came from coarse Polish village Jews. Our home, though, as far back as I can remember, was full of the new and old learning and was nouveau riche, and so we kept ourselves at a distance from Grandfather's simple village family. They were beneath us.

Grandfather's family must have been very common indeed. The uncles and cousins smacked of this lowly origin. People whispered to one another that my grandfather's father – whose name I heard only when he was called for the sixth Torah reading on Saturdays[1] – was a dairy farmer in a village near Kernizh.[2] My grandfather was the son of his father's first wife. I've never learned either what Grandfather's home was like or much about

---

1 The practice of reading the Law (Torah) every Sabbath is an ancient one. The Torah is taken from the ark and carried around the synagogue. Then seven persons are called to the reading. These calls (sing. *aliyah*, pl. *aliyot*) are considered an honour, but the third and the sixth *aliyot* are especially highly valued and are allotted to men of special learning and piety.
2 The Yiddish name of Kiernozia, a small town eighty kilometres northwest of Warsaw. All the names in the text are given in the form chosen by Trunk and, if necessary, explained in the footnotes.

his youth, only that he spent it among the peasants and Gentile girls of Kernizh. We swept that whole past under the carpet. Things were probably pretty much vulgar, village, and peasant-style. Grandfather Borukh in his youth must have been a bit of a natural man. Later, though, after he became wealthy, he studied the Talmud and wore a long silk coat on the Sabbath. For the Jewish New Year he travelled to his Hasidic rabbi; he took his place at the rabbi's table among the prominent guests and rabbis; and for those occasions, he wore a fur shtreimel hat.

Grandfather Borukh early on left his dairyman parental home and went to the neighbouring shtetl, Kernizh. There he fell in with Hasidim who gave him instruction, and he became a bit of a Torah scholar. He used to tell of how when a boy he was taken along by the Vurker[3] Hasidim of Kernizh to R. Mendel Vurker.[4] He travelled with them in a big covered wagon. Often and with great pleasure did he tell of that long Hasidic trip to the Vurker rabbi. All along the way, as the covered wagon strained slowly over sandy Polish roads, the Hasidim constantly danced for joy. In all the roadside inns little feasts were held, and the barrels of liquor, which were brought along all the way from Kernizh, had to be refilled again and again with whisky. Grandfather Borukh was a good storyteller. His tales had style, colour, and folksy fantasy. He gave the trip the feel of a pilgrimage to Jerusalem, and he always stressed, with pride, that he, the poor common lad, was taken on this ecstatically joyous Hasidic trip to the Vurker rabbi!

Grandmother Khaye, Grandfather Borukh's wife, came from a respectable well-to-do family from Żychlin.[5] Both her parents died of cholera in the course of one week. She was left a poor orphan. An aunt felt sorry for her and took her in. At home we did not talk of that part of Grandmother's past, and I can only

---

3 From Warka; in Yiddish, Vurke; a small town in central Poland on the Pilica River fifty kilometres south of Warsaw.

4 R. means 'rabbi' and should be used for actual ordained rabbis holding official positions. 'Reb' is an honorific used for all Jewish men in Yiddish, especially when only the first name is used.

5 A small town in the Kutno district sixty kilometres north of Łódź.

guess that Grandmother Khaye must have become a simple servant at that aunt's home. In her youth my grandmother must have been a great beauty. In her old age (she died in her eighties) she still bore traces of her former beauty. Her pale face had uncommonly regular features, and her skin was pale with a glimmer of a former noble delicacy. The poor orphan from Żychlin had a classic Greek nose.

Grandmother was as quiet as a dove. My grandfather must not have loved her very much. He frequently yelled at her and never showed her any tenderness or ever gave her so much as a good word. This further depressed her. She moved around the house with a truly Jewish woman's humbleness, forever in fear of Grandfather. Despite his overbearing treatment of her, she loved him with the quiet love of a Jewish woman who does not mull things over but sets aside her feelings according to the commands of the Torah. She never addressed Grandfather by his name. Everybody in the house ruled over her. Grandmother Khaye had many features of a pious Jewish woman. She was God-fearing and her charitable deeds were anonymous. She was superstitious like a true child of the common people and had a naive faith in Hasidic rabbis and in dragons. She also had an absurd faith in doctors, in all sorts of remedies and medicines. Everything that transcended reason and that seemed to have power over luck, health, and human life had an odd power over the feeling of inferiority of Grandmother Khaye. Showing itself either in the form of a quiet reserved goodness or in the form of powerless resignation, the feeling of inferiority was deeply embedded in the heart of this quiet woman who never had a happy life and who always depended on the kindness and the will of others.

The marriage of Grandmother Khaye and Grandfather Borukh must have been seen as a misalliance by her family. Hers was a respectable lower-middle-class family and my grandfather was, after all, a 'dairy boy.' My grandmother was left a helpless poor orphan, though, and the aunt for whom she worked as a maid wanted desperately to 'veil her head' and marry her off to a breadwinner.

After the wedding, my grandfather opened a shop in Sanik[6] and he did well. The estates in Sanik belonged to a great Polish magnate, Duke Sapieha. He liked Grandfather, who became his 'little Jew,' his *Żydek*, and remained the duke's favourite until the duke's death. After my grandfather himself had become a multi-millionaire, he still mentioned the duke's name with great respect, noting that he – the duke, that is – addressed Grandfather as 'my Berek' and even took him along in his lordly coach. While working for the duke, Grandfather accumulated property and leased villages from him. Later on, my grandfather bought his own estate, called Osmólsk, not far from Sanik and built himself a courtly palace and became a Jewish nobleman.

I was born on the estate of Osmólsk.

While still living in Sanik, Grandfather and Grandmother had several children but they all died in childhood. Neither Grandfather nor Grandmother ever spoke of their dead children and never mentioned them, probably for superstitious reasons. In all, they were left with one living daughter and this was my mother.

The fear and trembling with which my mother, the only surviving child, was brought up knew no bounds. She was taken to Hasidic rabbis so that they would bless her. With much piety and a shaking voice, Grandmother Khaye told of her journey with her only surviving child to the *tsadik*[7] of Gostynin[8] (the one described by Shalom Asch[9] in his novel *Salvation*, or *Der Tehilim Yid*), and the holy man from Gostynin placed his saintly hands on the little girl's head (not before her head was covered by a kerchief; only then would the rabbi place his hands on the heads of women) and blessed the surviving girl-child. My grandmother added that she had cried her heart out for the child before the Holy Sages.

---

6 In Polish, Sanniki; a village located twenty-five kilometres northeast of Żychlin.
7 A Hasidic rabbi.
8 A town located seventy-five kilometres north of Łódź and twenty kilometres north of Żychlin.
9 An outstanding Yiddish novelist and playwright (1880–1957) from the town of Kutno, located in the region that constitutes a scene of the Trunk story.

This was about the time when Grandfather Borukh was already the owner of Osmolin.[10] But not so quickly did the poor 'dairy boy' adapt to the idea that he was a privileged man, an estate owner, and that Osmolin bordered the estate of Duke Sapieha. A neighbour of Sapieha! Even as a rich man, my grandfather did not really change his old ways; he remained a common village Jew and had no other idea of this world of sensual pleasures than good garlic borscht with potatoes. Already the owner of the Osmolin estate, he still had no clear idea of how one goes about being aristocratic and since he could not get used to gentility – Grandfather was quaintly forthright – he put on none of the airs of a newly rich man. He did not act like a rich man and continued to live among his old Jewish friends of his younger years, that is, when he was a poor dairy farmer.

My grandfather ran the Osmólsk estate and at the same time continued to buy more estates and forests. His wealth grew, yet he himself continued to live in one poor room, at the home of a Jewish peasant, Simkhe Gayge. Grandmother Khaye raised chickens and geese. A quiet, unassuming woman, she had not the slightest ambition to put on the airs of a rich lady and she remained the obedient doormat to a strong man, whom she never addressed by name. Grandmother secretly sent donations to all the minor Hasidic rabbis and opened her little nest egg of money to all sorts of shady religious types who were criss-crossing Poland in their little wagons. Unable to make distinctions, she superstitiously believed that anybody wearing a shtreimel had superior power. She herself travelled to the greater and better-known *tsadikim* of Poland and did so with Grandfather's knowledge. Mainly, she travelled to the holy *tsadik* of Gostynin and to the holy *tsadik* Yankele of Radzymin,[11] for Grandfather Borukh was an ardent follower of the *tsadik* of Radzymin, to whose blessing he ascribed his fortune. Anxious Grandmother Khaye cooked pots of victuals for the poor and had only one thing in mind: to save her only daughter from the Angel of Death.

---

10 Another village near Sanniki.
11 A town on the eastern outskirts of Warsaw.

Chapter Two

R. Yoshua Kutner. His mother. Uncle Nathan-Meir, the ne'er-do-well. Grandmother Prive. The Hasidic merrymaker, Uncle Yekl. Uncle Yekl as a vinegar producer. On Purim Uncle Yekl crows like a cock and does somersaults for Yoshua Kutner. Uncle Yekl's 'clever' ideas. Aunt Shifra-Mirele. Grandfather Moyshl.

On my father's side I come from a most distinguished lineage. The distinction is twofold. One of the sides was scholarly and the other was Hasidic rabbinical.

My father's grandfather was the well-known gaon[1] R. Yoshua Kutner.[2] Reb Yoshua was the most popular Talmudic authority of his time. His name was known in the whole Diaspora of Israel. He was the ultimate *posek*,[3] and the most difficult Talmudic questions were sent to him for consideration from every corner of the world. Even today his name is legendary and I have met Sephardic Jews in faraway Morocco who mentioned his name with great respect.

---

1 A title given to outstanding scholars, often directing Talmudic academies.
2 A district town fifty kilometres from Łódź, the capital of the region where Żychlin, Kernizh, Sanniki, Osmólsk, and Osmolin are located. Jews were known both by family names and by place names. Thus R. Yehoshuale Trunk was R. Yehoshuale Kutner or R. Yoshua.
3 A specialist in the legal codes of the Torah who responds to difficult *halakhic* questions of Jewish law.

R. Yoshua was the most eminent branch of our family tree, the first ring of our chain of genealogy. I remember him from when I was still a child. When he died, I was six years old. Such was the respect felt by everyone around him that even a child was not insensible to it. Everyone seemed to tremble for his well-being and the household was proud of his fame, although the women of the household had no clear idea of what it involved. Scholars who knew him and told about him said that he spoke very fast, shot out short quotations, and only the very learned could understand and keep up with him in a Talmudic dispute. I remember him as an old man with a grey beard, sunken in a big leather rabbinical armchair.

R. Yoshua was extremely popular with the orthodox Jewish masses all over the world. But among the common unlearned people of Kutno, where he fulfilled the function of rabbi, his lustre was great and they told many stories about their holy man. In our family many legends grew around his person, his roots, and his boyhood. His mother, Deborah, was a poor, common orphan in Płock.[4] She was a pedlar standing in the market square and that was her livelihood. When from standing in the cold and in the heat she had saved a dowry – and she was a girl getting on in years by then – she went to the then rabbi of Płock, R. Leybush Khoref.[5] She showed him the hard-earned few rubles and asked that he, Rabbi Leybush Khoref, find her a husband, a Talmud scholar. The rabbi is said to have answered her that in Płock he knew an older man, a great Talmud scholar, and this was a poor *melamed*,[6] a bitter pauper but a great scholar. Moreover, the scholar, Reb David, was also a widower with several children, always struggling and barely able to support himself. The girl Deborah asked Rabbi Leybush Khoref whether the poor *melamed* in question was really a great Talmud scholar. 'Yes, my child, he is a very great Talmud scholar,' R. Leybush Khoref answered. Deborah, overworked and tired out, asked for no respite, and

---

4 A town on the River Vistula, one hundred kilometres northwest of Warsaw.
5 Yiddish-Hebrew for sharp-witted, very bright; from the Hebrew *harif*.
6 A teacher in a *kheyder*, a Jewish primary school.

with joy she undertook to marry the poor old man who was a great Talmud scholar. She had only a single child with the Talmudic scholar and that was R. Yoshua Kutner.

R. Yoshua was still a child when he became famous throughout Poland as an extraordinary prodigy. A wealthy Jewish family in Płock took this impoverished gifted young man in as a son-in-law.

I remember Grandmother Prive, the wife of R. Yoshua, extremely well. I was a grown-up boy when she died. She came from a very well-to-do family. We only know about her mother, Grandmother Ratse. Grandmother Ratse was a grandchild of Itshele Płotsker, one of the greatest Jewish magnates of old Poland. Reb Itshele's father, Shmuel Lasker, owned the Polish mint; that is, he smelted silver and gold coins for the Polish government. Reb Shmuel was sentenced to death because a weighing showed that silver which the Polish government had given him to be minted was missing. He was saved from death by a miracle. In our family it was said that because Reb Shmuel spent all his time at study and prayer, he had no time to oversee his men and that was why the silver weighing was short. A brother of Reb Shmuel was a wandering mystic and the author of a well-known Kabbalah[7] book.

But let me return to Grandmother Ratse. It seems that she was the main person in business and the mistress of the house. Her name appears prominently in the family annals. Her husband, Grandfather Reb Chaim, was kept in the shadow. I should imagine that Grandmother Ratse's husband could have been of no high masculine or spiritual quality. Evidence of this was his two sons, the uncles, that is, the hefty brothers of Grandmother Prive.

I did not know these two uncles personally. They died before I was born, but the family talked about them over and over again. My father told terribly funny stories about one of them, Uncle Nathan-Meir. Uncle Nathan's mental development would seem to have been arrested. His life was full of funny incidents stem-

---

7 An esoteric Jewish philosophy based on the mystical interpretation of the Scriptures.

ming from his mental retardation and disorientation. My father told the following stories about Uncle Nathan-Meir.

Uncle Nathan-Meir was in the habit of travelling around Poland. How he covered the expense of these jaunts is not known. He used to come to his brother-in-law, Reb Yoshua Kutner, for help. In Kutno he would spend several weeks, sleep in the *sukkah*,[8] spend whole days in a state of depression, in stony silence. Should his deliberation result in actual speech, it was always unsuited for the occasion. Uncle Nathan was forever making blunders, and they resulted in the funniest of situations. He was a tall lanky man, and yet it seemed to him perfectly sensible to try to put on a child's coat. When the coat did not fit, he would tug at it vigorously and then loudly proclaim his wonder that somehow he had outgrown it.

Uncle Nathan-Meir also chronically missed trains. This too had a funny side to it. The approaching train would whistle, frightening him badly so that he had to urinate. Before he could unbutton and rebutton himself, wash his hands, and say the blessing after using the toilet, which took quite a while for an efficient person like Uncle Nathan to say, the train had gone. And so when, after a long stay at his sister's, he finally decided to go home, it still took him many weeks to go. This because the ill-starred story of the train whistle, the fright, and the answering the call of nature repeated itself over and again, and Uncle Nathan could not get moving. My father told me that during one such long period of the train problem, clever people advised him – Uncle Nathan, that is – to go to the train station some ten hours before the departure of the train, in order to become used to the whistling of other trains and thus not to become frightened and to avoid all the consequences of the call of nature and finally to be able to get himself out of Kutno. The advice delighted him. Next morning, some ten hours before the departure of the train, he got into a feverish hurry to catch it. In his great haste he

---

8 A booth built for the holiday of Sukkot (the Feast of Tabernacles), a celebration of the dwellings during the Israelites' wandering in the desert.

knocked his head against a cupboard. Uncle Nathan then stayed on in Kutno for weeks in bed with a split head. Then it was that he uttered the profound truth that nothing good comes from haste. This uttering of a logical aphorism was a novelty for Uncle Nathan, who was never able to fit the right word into the right situation. And my father told me that that was the only apt word Uncle Nathan-Meir ever said.

One more story our family used to tell about Uncle Nathan-Meir. Uncle Nathan-Meir had a daughter. While at his rabbi's on Rosh Hashanah,[9] he arranged for the engagement of the girl with another Hasid. On returning home, he forgot to mention that he had betrothed the girl. Next year he was again at his rabbi's table, and there he fixed with the prospective bride's father the date of the wedding. And again he said not a word about it at home. One fine day there rolled into the market of his shtetl a wagon loaded with wedding guests, maternal and paternal. The groom, wan from fasting on his wedding day, wore a new cap and a new wedding coat. The covered wagon of family guests and playing fiddlers arrived at Uncle Nathan-Meir's house assuming that a klezmer[10] orchestra would meet them and that food for the wedding dishes was simmering away in pots. How dumbfounded they were to find that Uncle Nathan-Meir's family had not only not even the faintest notion that today was the wedding day but that they were also not even aware that the girl was engaged to be married. The women of the groom's family gazed at the would-be bride and were dismayed. The girl, dirty and dishevelled, was just then standing in the middle of the room sweeping the floor with a broom. Panic reigned. The groom nearly fell in a swoon from fasting and dishonour. Inquiries were made for the whereabouts of the clever perpetrator of the deed, that is, the crook, the father of the bride, Nathan-Meir. It turned out that Uncle Nathan-Meir happened to be away from home. He had taken a notion to pay his rabbi a visit. Many more stories were

---

9 The Jewish New Year.
10 Yiddish for a musician.

told in the family about Uncle Nathan-Meir, who was never on time and always did the wrong thing at the wrong time.

More grotesque and wonderful stories were told in the family about Uncle Nathan-Meir, who was ever late and ever doing things the wrong way. At the time when I was listening to them as they were being told, Uncle Nathan-Meir had already passed on to the luminous Garden of Eden a good forty years earlier at least. Nevertheless, he was remembered on occasions. And there were opportunities galore because every Trunk is bemused and quite hapless. We had an adage in the family that there is a bit of Uncle Nathan-Meir in every Trunk. And as for myself, there is much of Uncle Nathan-Meir in me. In the family of Grandmother Prive there was an extraordinary amount of Uncle Nathan-Meir.

I remember Grandmother Prive when she was very old and R. Yoshua Kutner's widow. She remains in my memory as a bent and small old woman with bad eyes and a lace cap on her head. She sat in an armchair putting moist cotton wool to her eyes. Earlier, during the Kutner's lifetime, she was the mistress of the house and very energetic. She was not excessively kind. She played her role with a strong hand. Her only concern and aim in life was to protect her husband. In that way she believed that she was zealously sustaining the source of the Torah. When R. Yoshua died and his body was lying on the floor, she came close to him and uncovered the great man's body and said to the corpse's face that in the other world he was to remember she had a share in his Torah.

R. Yoshua Kutner had three children. He had one son, who later became the rabbi of Kutno and was the father of my father, and also two daughters.

The eldest was Aunt Sarah (or Sorel). Aunt Sorel was an extraordinarily pious woman, unassuming and a woman of the people. Although the daughter of the *gaon* of Kutno, she mingled with the simplest folk. She was much loved in the town. Her husband, Uncle Yekl, was small and pudgy and a comic figure. First of all, he was a wild Hasidic reveller. In his youth he used to spend whole days partying and wanted no part in any business. Just once in his life he gave in to pressure to start a vinegar

factory. This did not last long. The Hasidim drank the alcohol
that was bought for the factory. Uncle Yekl poured plain water on
wood chips hoping to produce vinegar in a miraculous way. The
miracle did not take place, and to his great satisfaction, Uncle
Yekl was no longer an industrialist but reverted to the old
bohemian Hasidic revelry. Aunt Sorel opened a little shop of
sewing goods, odds and ends, kept Uncle Yekl out of it, and in
such a way supported herself through her own hard work. How
much truth there is in the story of the water on the chips I do not
know, but it is entirely in keeping with Uncle Yekl's whole being.
His days of glory were Simchat Torah[11] and Purim.[12] Especially
Purim. Then Uncle Yekl was on the highest level. For the two days
before and the two days after Purim, Uncle Yekl was unrecognizable. His face blackened with soot, his coat turned inside out, he
danced with Hasidim in the streets of Kutno and had the friendly
and happy nerve of visiting his father-in-law dressed in such an
outfit. R. Yoshua, forever busy with the Torah, had neither the
humour nor the understanding for such silly Hasidic pranks. R.
Yoshua had no love for Uncle Yekl, first of all because he, Uncle
Yekl, was a ne'er-do-well, not overly bright, and was unconcerned
about the whole burden of making a living, which rested on the
shoulders of frail Aunt Sorel. Then, Uncle Yekl was also no
scholar of the Torah, which did not improve his standing with his
father-in-law, the Gaon. Uncle Yekl knew this and felt himself to
be despised and unrespected by his father-in-law. On Purim,
though, the boot was on the other foot. During Purim, Uncle
Yekl felt superior to all the learned and scholarly. Purim is the
heyday for merry Jews. Singing, dishevelled in an inside-out coat
with a gang of dancing dishevelled Hasidim – no scholars either
– Uncle Yekl would burst in on R. Yoshua with a bright and cheerful 'Happy Purim.' First of all, Uncle Yekl turned a somersault
right in front of R. Yoshua Kutner, sitting there majestically in his

11 The Festival of the Rejoicing of the Law, three weeks after Rosh Hashanah.
12 A Jewish festival of joy celebrated to commemorate the deliverance of Persian Jews
from the evil plans of Haman, the chief minister of King Ahasveros. It falls one
month before the spring holiday of Passover.

leather armchair engrossed in study. Then Uncle Yekl would – of all things – crawl up on top of the wood stove and from there, crow like a cock.

This was the only day, Purim, when the Hasidic bohemia, with Uncle Yekl at the top of the tree, by legal sanction dominated the rabbi's study of Yoshua Kutner. After Purim, everything fizzled like a burned-out campfire, and Uncle Yekl was quiet and meek, once more beneath the contemptuous treatment of Yoshua Kutner, and celebrated Hasidic banquets at home under the aegis of good-natured Aunt Sorel. In other ways, too, Uncle Yekl was an odd character. First of all, he always had secrets. What secrets could such a good-for-nothing reveller as Uncle Yekl have had? A psychologist might have a ready answer: namely, that the uncle would create a secret from the smallest trifle is psychologically understandable by his wish to elevate himself out of the muck of inferiority and from being a classic good-for-nothing. On an occasion of a 'secret,' Uncle Yekl would call one away to an empty room and ask if his interlocutor had some toilet paper or other such 'secrets,' in which Uncle Yekl would stress the importance of his needs. Moreover, Uncle Yekl was a person with a 'rational mind.' Since it was taken for granted that in practical matters the advice of a pitiable revelling beggar like Uncle Yekl is not sought after by anyone, Uncle Yekl pressed his advice, whether he was asked for it or not.

Above all, Uncle Yekl shone with advice when a wedding was being prepared in the family and the wedding was to take place in another town and so it was necessary to travel by train. Travel? Well, Uncle Yekl would start putting together advance plans. Should it turn out that there was a good connection to the other town and the whole trip should take no more than two hours, Uncle Yekl, using 'common sense,' would work out that one needed to travel two days and two nights, leave Kutno at three o'clock in the morning and reach the other town after several days at four o'clock in the morning, without eating, drinking, or sleeping. The master plan rested on the ability to eat at five o'clock in the morning before praying. Exactly what is commonly called 'common sense'! It goes without saying that no one paid the slightest attention to Uncle Yekl, but he stood firm.

The second daughter of R. Yoshua was Aunt Shifra-Mirele, the one called the 'rebetsn[13] of Kalisz.'[14] As opposed to the modesty and simplicity of Aunt Sorel, Aunt Shifra-Mirele boasted of her pedigree and did not forget for a moment that she was the daughter of Reb Yoshua Kutner. Besides that, her style of domesticity was the opposite of Aunt Sorel's family life. Aunt Shifra-Mirele's first marriage was held by the family under seven veils. The case was as follows. Her father, R. Yoshua Kutner, had contracted a marriage with a rich Jew from Warsaw. The young man from Warsaw didn't appreciate the scholarly tenor of R. Yoshua's home. He was unimpressed by either the scholarship or the genealogical descent. One fine day he was off to Berlin, as it would appear, with a *shikse*.[15] There was much shame and disgrace, and the young man was hurriedly given a divorce. Nor was the young man much shaken by it.

Aunt Shifra-Mirele was left a sixteen-year-old divorcee. She was soon married to one of the best-known rabbis in Poland, the rabbi of Kalisz, R. Chaim Eliezer Wachs, the author of the book *The Living Soul* (*Nefesh Haya*). He was a man in his late forties and a widower with a number of children. From then on, the golden era began in Aunt Shifra-Mirele's life. Her snobbery over pedigree found the right ground on which to play itself out. The rabbi of Kalisz had marriage connections with the richest people in Poland. Aunt Shifra-Mirele was steeped in dignity and in velvet. When I knew her, she had already come down from her kingdom, she was a widow of the 'Living Soul.' Later on, R. Yoshua Kutner married her off to a rich man in Łódź, Shimon Tsilikh, a strange person of whom I shall have more to say later. Aunt Shifra-Mirele was left a widow with two daughters by the rabbi of Kalisz and was always afterwards called 'the Kalisher *rebetsn*.' She had a big tummy, a thick red nose, and always

---

13 In Yiddish a rabbi's wife.
14 A large town in central Poland one hundred kilometres west of Łódź.
15 A derogatory Yiddish word for a Gentile girl.

remembered who she was, what her descent was, and her station at the side of the 'Living Soul.'

My grandfather Moyshl – that is, my father's father – was the only son of R. Yoshua Kutner. Grandfather was a tall, wonderfully handsome man with the majestic appearance of a Slavic prince. The silk attire of a rabbi, the fur-trimmed hat, and the watch case lent him no Jewish appearance; on the contrary, they added to the Slavic element, as in the paintings of Matejko[16] and Repin.[17] It was said that in his appearance my father's father resembled the magnate grandfathers of Grandmother Prive.

His character, which I will come to later on, was a very strange and complicated one. Add to this the fact that for several years in his youth after his marriage he was afflicted by a severe mental illness. The years of grandfather's 'night of the soul' were kept secret in my family. It was only whispered about miracles that had happened and how he became well. The 'night of the soul' would seem to have been a severe illness with very serious complications. In any event, in his later years, he became well and fit for action. He was rabbi for the shtetl of Wiskitno,[18] and after R. Yoshua's death, he took over the rabbinical chair of Kutno. Grandfather spent much time in study, and drank much wine at joyous occasions and Hasidic feasts. After the death of the Hasidic rabbi of Aleksandrów,[19] the so-called Let Israel Rejoice (Yismah Israel), he was one of the foremost candidates to be the new rabbi. He declined. I intend to describe his character in further volumes, when I describe my grandfather as I personally knew him. Much of his stiff-necked stubbornness was a result of that 'night of the soul.'

---

16 Jan Matejko (1838–93), a Polish painter whose huge historical pictures illustrate the Polish past.
17 Ilya Efimovich Repin (1844–1930), a Russian painter and the most famous member of the Realist group.
18 A village on the southern outskirts of Łódź.
19 A town just northwest of Łódź.

Chapter Three

Grandmother Leah. The Hasidim of Vurke. Hasidic journeys to Vurke. The Young Vurker. Reb Yoshel Prager. Grandmother Leah's wedding in Praga. Grandfather Moyshl becomes ill. Grandmother Leah in an attic chamber next to the women's shtibl *of Kutno. She reads storybooks in Yiddish. Joy of children.*

Grandmother Leah, Grandfather's wife and the daughter-in-law of the Kutner, came from a great rabbinic lineage. Her mother's father was the noted R. Yitshok Vurker and her father's father was R. Yoshel Prager.

Yitshok Vurker was one of the apostles of Polish Hasidism. He was the antipode of the Kotsker rebbe.[1] The Kotsker rested Hasidism on the solitary and on the individual. To the Kotsker the whole world was no more than a piece of matter. Humanity was a chunk of this world matter. Only a solitary personality can extricate itself, after great inner struggles, from world materialism and be free and elevated. The ideal of the Kotsker was no more than 'ten Jews standing on all rooftops and shouting: God is King.' The world can be saved only in a single person. The world and humanity can never go out beyond the circle of materiality. They must stay in it forever. In modern philosophy the

---

1 From Kock (sometimes spelled Kotsk), a town located sixty kilometres north of Lublin.

Kotsker's ideas might be compared to Nietzsche's and Schopen-
hauer's. They also viewed the world as the manifestation of an
inert and low will, and only a genius or a superman can, in a
wonderful and laborious way, rise above the dark and bestial fate
of the world. It is the road towards the ultimate misanthropic
pessimism.

The Vurker's outlook was exactly the opposite and sprang from
a completely optimistic viewpoint; namely, that the original
sources of the world were a great love; that is, a great feeling of
commonality. The low and the evil are only lapses in a peaceful
world harmony. Every human being is in essence a divine sub-
stance, and if only the person wishes, he can easily return to the
source of the world. The Vurker's love for all people is proverbial
even today among Polish Hasidim. A love that was heightened by
world wisdom and world knowledge. The Kotsker said that the
Vurker 'slouches around heaven with his boots on'; that is, that
he, R. Yitshok Vurker, sees there, in the highest elevations of life,
a place for everyone.

Grandmother Leah was R. Yitshok Vurker's grandchild, a
daughter of his daughter. The Vurker's daughter, my Grandmother Blimele, was an extraordinary woman and a great personality. I knew her well. In the next volumes I intend to tell
much about her.

Grandmother Blimele's first husband was the son of R. Yoshel
Prager. Yoshel Prager was one of the best-known Polish rabbis
and the author of the book *Behold in the Heavens*. His son, R.
Avremele, was the rabbi of Białobrzegi.[2] He died young in Vurka
at the house of the Vurker's son, R. Mendel, the so-called Young
Rebbe.[3] That was what Hassidim called him as opposed to his
father, R. Yitshok, who was called the Old Rebbe.

After the death of her father, R. Avremele, Grandmother Leah
stayed on at the house of my grandfather, R. Yoshel Prager. Her
mother, Grandmother Blimele, soon married R. Zalmen Shepser,

---

2 A small town fifteen kilometres southwest of Warka.
3 Affectionate Yiddish pronunciation of 'rabbi,' used for a beloved teacher or Hasidic
  leader.

a noted rabbi and one of the respected Hasidim of Vurke. Grandmother Leah and her older sister, Aunt Rachel, were brought up
at Yoshel Prager's. At a very early age, Grandmother Leah was
betrothed to my grandfather, Moshe Pinchas, the only son of the
Kutner.

The wedding took place in Praga[4] at R. Yoshel's. Many decades
later, the old Jews of Warsaw told of the wedding. R. Yoshel was
then in his nineties. Frail with age, he spent most of the time in
bed and from his bed continued to function as a rebbe with the
Hasidim. R. Yoshel was said to have had much humour, and the
humour did not leave him in bed, where he lay, a frail but fully
mentally alert old man. All the Hasidic rebbes and the best-
known rabbis of Poland came to the wedding. What else could
one expect when the Kutner celebrates a wedding with R. Yoshel
Prager!

The wedding was compared to the great joyous rabbinical
events, which abide in the memory of the Polish Hasidim. Next
to the groom at the head of the table sat R. Yoshua Kutner. From
the bride's side were Yoshel Prager (who because of his age could
sit at the table only with an effort) and the bride's uncles, the two
sons of R. Yitshok Vurker, R. David Amshinover and R. Mendel,
the Young Vurker.

As Hasidim tell it, the Young Vurker had the stately appearance
of royalty. A tall, big-boned man, he had a long majestic beard. In
the white silken garment ornamented with silver hooks, he shone
among the others like an apparition from a higher world. The
Hasidim who used to travel to him – many of them I knew personally in my youth – continued for decades after his death to
talk about him with a moving and rare love. Their eyes lit up as
soon as they started talking about the Young Vurker.

The Young Vurker was taciturn by nature, spoke but seldom,
but every word that came out of his mouth reflected a great inner
spirituality. He spoke in aphorisms, and just like the Kotsker, he
too used hardly any Hebrew words. His love for God was full of

---

4 A part of Warsaw located on the right bank of the River Vistula.

deep enthusiasm and his silent love for people stemmed from the same exhilaration. The Hasidim told how they physically felt an indescribable love that emanated from the Young Vurker. Everyone who came near this radius of love felt inwardly elevated.

Hasidim talked about the journeys to the Young Vurker as though of the happy pilgrimages to ancient Jerusalem. When the covered wagons of travelling Hasidim were nearing the fields of Vurke, they were overtaken by a Hasidic fervour, which turned into a Hasidic dance. There was dancing in the wagons, in the inns, and in the fields. In the inn immediately before Vurke, in the village of Kiner,[5] they enacted out and out Hasidic ecstasies. Barrels of liquor were opened and a feeling prevailed of religious ecstatic Hasidic togetherness. And they danced. The Young Vurker would often go to meet them himself at the inn in Kiner. His love and his inner longing for the Jews who were making their way up the roads towards Vurke shone. For it was by no means customary for a rebbe to travel out to meet his Hasidim. The Vurker's longing was exceptionally great and was always reaching out to the longing of others, like sources to sources. In general terms the Vurker's manner could be described as an endless dynamic love and a dynamic soulful, unquenchable longing.

At the wedding in Praga, the Young Vurker was sitting at the end of a table among the great rabbis and rebbes. As Hasidim tell it, his presence shone like a heavenly vision as he sat there, black-bearded and dressed in a white silk garment. He sat next to the brilliant R. Yoshua of Kutno and was wonderfully silent while the Kutner swam in the sea of the Talmud and dazzled the greatest rabbis with his scholarly brilliance. Then the young rebbe of Vurka shot a question at the rabbi of Kutno: 'Kutner rabbi, what is the meaning of "When Once We Walked Together?"'

In his youth the Kutner had been in Kotsk, idolized the holy man of Gostynin, and had deep sympathy for Hasidism. He well understood what this question of the Young Vurker's meant,

---

5 The Yiddish name for the village of Konary, nine kilometres north of Warka.

which was that in a word that every Jew understands and can readily use there is inherent much more spiritual depth than in all the edifices of erudition. And with great empathy for what was in the young rebbe's mind, he returned the question.

'And you, rebbe of Vurke, what do you think is the meaning of "When once we walked together?"' Thereupon 'One means one and only,' came the young rebbe of Vurke's reply. With that he meant to express the great pantheistic feeling which burned so strongly in his soul and which was the essence of his feeling of love.

Such, then, were the tales and remarks that the old Hasidim of Warsaw loved to tell decades after Grandmother Leah's wedding.

For a short time after the wedding the young couple boarded with Reb Avrom Prager. Then they moved over to Kutno to live with her father-in-law, the Kutner.

The couple were in fact still children, and Grandmother Leah told me that with Grandfather Moyshl – her husband, that is – they played in the sand in R. Yoshua's yard in Kutno. The couple also played with all the *kheyder* boys. This aroused the anger of the strict and non-whimsical Grandmother Prive, who told them off severely.

And in almost the sixteenth year of her life Grandmother Leah became pregnant with my father.

Many were the times when Grandmother Leah told me of those days. She lived in a small attic room next to the women's synagogue[6] of Kutno. She was very sad. The granddaughter of the rebbe of Vurke, who was brought up in the simple love of Israel and among Hasidic merrymakers, felt out of place in the high seriousness of the rabbinic gaonic home of the Kutner. Here they smiled but rarely. The only merrymaker in the family, Uncle Yekl, came to visit his father-in-law only occasionally. The Kutner had little love for him. Only on Purim and Simchat Torah did Uncle Yekl feel that his merriness did not play second fiddle to his father-

---

6 The custom was for women to pray separately from men in the women's section, the *vayber-shul* or *shtibl*, which might be a balcony or a separate room with a window opening onto the men's *shul* (synagogue in Yiddish).

in-law's erudition. On Purim and Simchat Torah even the Master of the Universe stays at a little distance from the dry Gemara[7] and he prefers the company of Hasidic revellers. And so Uncle Yekl would in fact drop in to the dusty book-filled study of his brilliant father-in-law, with a gang of tipsy revellers with a loud and cheery '*Gut-Yontef.*'[8] Uncle Yekl was a Hasid in Vurke, and he alone reminded Grandmother Leah of her vanished childhood years. The good Aunt Sorel was busy all day working for a living. The proud *rebetsn* of Kalisz reigned over her realm alongside the rabbi of Kalisz. She came to Kutno but seldom. And even when she did come, she saw in the modest rabbinical genealogy of Grandmother Leah a challenge to the distinction of her own father, the Gaon, and her husband, the rabbi of Kalisz. The *rebetsn* looked down her nose at a heritage that did not derive from rabbinical learning and deep rabbinical leather armchairs. Not much of a pedigree, to descend from people whose words can be grasped by common *arendars*[9] (lease-holders) and for which no honed intellect is needed. Grandmother Prive was an earnest, humourless mother-in-law, always busy in the kitchen or in communal charitable matters, and the father-in-law, R. Yoshua, the world genius, swam majestically in the Sea of the Talmud. Grandmother Leah looked up to him as though to something incomprehensible with which a Jewish woman can have no common ground. Grandfather Moyshl, Grandmother's young husband, was away for whole nights in the Vurke prayer house, where he whooped it up all night with the Hasidim and snatched an occasional card game. Playing cards was also a part of the activities of Vurker Hasidim. It was said that playing cards brings the hearts of the players closer, fanning the flame of attachment and friendship. Thus it was that Grandmother Leah, in truth still a child and advanced in pregnancy, spent whole nights alone in the little attic room next to the women's *shul.* She was frightened, knowing that at midnight dead women gather in the adjoining *shtibl* to say prayers.

---

7 The Talmudic text elucidating the Mishna, the compilation of the Jewish oral law.
8 In Yiddish, 'Good holiday.'
9 A Jew leasing a mill, an inn, or any facility owned by a nobleman; Polish: *arendarz.*

Grandmother Leah was afraid to undress and lie down to sleep. She sat by the light of a cheap candle and waited for her young husband to return at last from the *shtibl.* In the meantime, by the pale light from the little penny candle, she began to read Yiddish storybooks. These storybooks written in Yiddish were authored by the first wave of the enlightened *maskil*[10] writers. These little books made a great impression on Grandmother Leah. They altered her outlook on life, disposing her to be critical of many accepted views. Those little Enlightenment booklets also determined the spiritual fate of the children born to Grandmother Leah later in life.

---

10 *Maskil* is Hebrew for an advocate of the Enlightenment.

Chapter Four

My father the prodigy. Satisfaction. My father writes poetry. R. Yoshua Kutner's manuscript.

And such was the frame of mind in which Grandmother Leah, herself still almost a child, gave birth to my father. Grandmother Leah used to tell me often: the baby was her only solace during those long nights when she sat all alone in the attic room next to the women's *shul* waiting for grandfather who was merrymaking with Hasidim in their *shtibl*. Here she read the Yiddish storybooks, which fell on her young and aching girl's heart as dew falls on arid ground. Or she looked at the little live being that amazingly had emerged from her womb. The child in the cradle was like an embodiment of her girlish dreams and longings in the dry and gloomy air of Reb Yoshua Kutner's home. This home's atmosphere was filled with the great baffling arcana of the Torah, which are not accessible to women and simple people, exactly the opposite of the Vurke Hasidic atmosphere.

Grandfather's first symptoms of the later 'night of the soul' must have appeared then. The uncanny, dark, and obsessed atmosphere that surrounds the dark and closed-off world of the 'night of the soul' must have been very frightening to the naive and by nature cheerful and poetic young girl. Vurke had been a fount of love and joy where a wondrous inner openness of the spirit prevailed, in contrast to the world in which Grandmother

Leah now found herself and where she spent the lonely night in the neighbourhood of dead women who turned up at midnight from the graveyard and keened their supplications in the empty women's section.

The baby in the cradle was slowly growing up. From the earliest childhood, it was showing extraordinary capabilities. Grandmother Leah was happy. A rumour was spreading that a wonder child, another R. Yoshua Kutner, was growing up. R. Yoshua himself was taking an interest in the brightness of the little grandchild and very early began to look after him. Thus it was that the Talmudic Gaon became closer to Grandmother Leah.

To tell now of the talents shown by my father in his childhood years, as they were recounted to me by others, would take me away from my theme. These were years of a Jewish boy genius growing up in a rabbinic home. While still a child, my father also wrote Hebrew poems patterned on the old Jewish Enlightenment writers, and R. Yoshua, who held poems in but little esteem, was nevertheless so very fond of this little grandchild of his that he showed the poems to his son-in-law, Shifra-Mirele's husband, the well-known Kalisz rabbi and the author of *The Living Soul*. The Kalisher was a well-known worldly rabbi who was reputed to have connections among the richest people in Poland. These affluent and far-reaching connections required stepping into the great world, the great halls of the rich, foreign watering places, silken princely dresses, expensive china and glass, gold and silver, and genuine Brussels lace. It was the great world, as opposed to the orthodox and rabbinic home of the Kutner, where tight-fisted Grandmother Prive set the tone of housekeeping. The rabbi of Kalisz also loved the delicate and gifted little boy. The rabbi of Kalisz was himself a writer in the high-flown ornate *melitse*[1] style, and his handwriting was small and fine, the exact opposite of the Gaon, who wrote in bold rabbinical style and his handwriting, with his script looking like wild drakes and shovels, was bad. He wrote his Torah novellae erratically spread all over the pages of the books in his library. It was necessary to find skilled copyists

---

1 An elegant Hebrew style full of aphorisms.

among the scholarly students of the *besmedresh*[2] who were able to find a way among these hieroglyphic inscriptions. The Kalisz rabbi praised the poems of my father before the Kutner. Yet I am convinced that the Gaon was much more pleased with my father's subtle casuistic interpretations. A sharp question, a poser, meant much more to R. Yoshua than all the charms of the Hebrew muse.

And so my father grew up, developed, and won a name across Poland for his precocity. The Kutner praised him and was steady in the admiration of his abilities. The poor maternal heart of the dreaming and intelligent Grandmother Leah was full of joy. Grandfather Moyshl was finally recognized as mentally ill. Grandmother Leah began to have more children. Her loneliness became deeper and her longings greater. She continued to dwell in the little attic room next to the women's *shul* and continued to have long sleepless nights rocking the children in cradles, reading the Yiddish storybooks written by Enlightenment writers, and watching her eldest son growing up and finding favour and sympathy in everybody's eyes and becoming the apple in his grandfather's eyes end slowly becoming a marriageable boy. Into the loneliness of Grandmother Leah's life slowly stole beams of joy from her children.

---

2 House of study; in Hebrew, Beit ha-Midrash.

Chapter Five

With the help of folk medicine and rebbes, my mother slowly grows to marriageable age. Simkhe Gayge the Jewish peasant. Simkhe Gayge with a priest during a storm in the forest. Sore Bine, Uncle Avromke, and Aunt Royze. Uncle Avromke lives in a shack. Aunt Royze rolled a Yom Kippur candle. The aura of Judgment Day. Uncle Mordekhai-Ber of the six fingers. Aunt Genendl. Their great brood of children. Uncle Mordekhai's tavern in Osmolin. Łowicz. Peasant men and women of Łowicz. Sunday in the fields. The annual market in Osmolin. Uncle Mordekhai-Ber dances with the peasants. Tisha B'Av and the minyan *in Osmolin. The ruins of Jerusalem. A synagogue trustee is appointed. Uncle Leyzer Yosef and Aunt Toybe. Uncle Leyzer Yosef tells of the Turkish war and of battles around Plevna. Uncle Yosef under Aunt Toybe's thumb. Uncle takes cover among the chickens.*

Under the trembling care of Grandmother Khaye and sustained by exorcisms, folk remedies, and blessings from rebbes at whose door Grandmother Khaye never ceased to knock, particularly the old Radzyminer and the Holy Man of Gostynin, her only child was growing up, the girl who was petitioned back from death, the little daughter who was to become my mother.

Grandfather Borukh Gzhivatsh, the landowner of Osmólsk, continued to live in the miserable shtetl of Osmolin in a rented room he occupied in the house of a Jewish peasant, Simkhe Gayge. Later, when I knew Simkhe, he was a rich man, owned a house in Łódź, and at the same time was employed by Grandfather as a forest overseer in Łagiewniki.[1] Grandfather took him now and then to the rebbe in Stryków.[2] Poor Simkhe had to put on a silken garment and a *shtreimel,* in which he looked like an actor playing a rebbe. Even when Simkhe 'had made it,' he still looked like a raw and primitive village Jew. He was a sturdy little man with a coarse voice and a hard little grey beard which, peasant-fashion, grew on his broad chin and on his thick and red neck. He had the upturned nose of a Gentile and burning reddish eyes. His hands were those of a hard-working man, hairy and with earth under the nails. As I remember him from Łagiewniki, Simkhe Gayge used to go about all day dressed like a peasant, in trousers and braces. He rose very early together with the Gentiles and the chickens. When he was not in the forest or in the sawmill, he hung out among the cows, the hens, and the goats. He smelt of barn dung. He was always quarrelling with the peasants and cursed them in their own tongue. He spoke the thick peasant dialect and felt more at home with them than with the rabbi of Stryków. Simkhe always carried a revolver with him, and his great pleasure was to shoot among the trees. He loved the echo of the revolver shot in the wood, the 'cuckoo' of the cuckoo bird, the lowing of cows, the cackle of geese and hens, the mysterious rustling of the old oak groves in Łagiewniki. The wind and the rain sounded more homey and reassuring to his raw and primeval spirit than the noble and sickly whines of the Hasidic rebbes to whom he was now and then taken by Grandfather Borukh. Like all the peasants, Simkhe too despised the pale and acculturated city Jews. Although a pious Jew, he liked to tell a story of how once he was caught by a storm in the wood when travelling with a priest and he spent the night covered by the priest's cassock. Lightning tore the skies, thunder rolled among the trees, rain rippled in the rustling darkness, and trees snapped in the storm. He and the priest huddled together under the

---

1 A village five kilometres north of Łódź, on the outskirts of Zgierz.
2 A little town fifteen kilometres northeast of Łódź.

cassock. The priest said a prayer and Simkhe, like an animal, was listening to the play of the elements. His wife, Sore Bine, a small stout woman with a faded yellow wig, trembled in his presence, and while so trembling, she bore his children, who were all as raw and hugely healthy as he was himself. Sore Bine paled when Simkhe would all of a sudden and for no reason glare at her with his reddish fiery eyes and then from under the bristling moustaches utter a heavy peasant curse-word.

Aside from Simkhe, there lived in Osmolin Grandfather's family, the healthy leaseholders, and their wives. I knew all of them. In order to describe the environment in which my grandfather lived and in which my mother was brought up and in which I was later born, I'll stop here to describe them.

Uncle Avromke was Grandfather Borukh's eldest brother. He was a small, thin man with a moulting little beard, with gaps on his chin, and with a long, red nose always covered by bluish, dried blotches. His nose was long and pointed and cut his face like a pointed board. Uncle Avromke was an intensely silent man but a merry Jew just the same. He held his head low and always looked at the floor, and he always shivered as though something were biting him. He had the greatest respect for his younger brother, the rich man and landowner of Osmolin. The respect was expressed in such a way that when he saw Grandfather Borukh, he would lower his head still further down, shiver even more, and become silent like a stone. Nor did Grandfather Borukh speak to him, although he loved him more than a little. When I was a child, Uncle Avromke lived in a big rectangular shack in the middle of the market of Osmolin, a house with a half-bowed, rotting shingled roof. In front of the door of this hovel stood an old dried-out butcher's block like a big altar. It was said that every now and again Uncle Avromke slaughtered a calf or a lamb and therefore was something of a butcher. He had a small frail wife, Aunt Royze; it seems to me that she was his second wife. She had a broad flat face covered with freckles and wore a sort of a cap with a bird on it. As I remember, Aunt Royze was always wrapped in a torn Turkish shawl and when she talked it seemed like the chirp of the bird on her cap. This sickly and odd couple flooded the world with kids, as though having a child was a duty exacted on every activity! Kids! From the womb of Aunt Royze streamed a host of sons and daughters, tall, healthy, and big-boned like oaks in the forest but all with large freckles on their faces, exactly like Aunt Royze. As soon as they grew up, they flew away from Uncle Avromke's hovel like pigeons away from a coop. Mostly they went to Łódź, became workers there, and were never bold enough to visit Grandfather Borukh. Just as they were healthy and tall, so they were also shy like peasant children. They were especially shy in the presence of Grandfather Borukh. They blushed and lowered their eyes. It was a peasant-like shyness and brought to mind red apples. Later, in the years 1905–6, Uncle Avromke's sons joined the Bund,[3] took part in the revolution, and fought on the barricades. From then on, the weak threads connecting them with our wealthy family were severed altogether and I never saw them anymore.

One episode with Aunt Royze is imprinted in my memory, and it happened on the eve of Yom Kippur.[4] We lived by then in the 'court' that Grandfather Borukh built in the middle of a large orchard. Grandmother Khaye put on the orange silk dress with lace which she never wore between one Yom Kippur and the next. I was a child and was taken by Grandmother to Uncle Avromke's hovel. I carried Grandmother's Yom Kippur prayer book. Aunt Royze and several other older women rolled the great waxen Yom Kippur candles. Aunt Royze, in her big Turkish shawl and with the bird on her cap, was busy. She looked like one of the witches in *Macbeth* in a folksy Yiddish edition. They all, including Grandmother Khaye, were standing around the table crying bitterly and saying prayers, and Aunt Royze angrily and bitterly rolled the yellow Yom Kippur candles as the dead body is turned on the purification board before burial. It felt like the Day of

---

3 The General Union (Bund) of Jewish Workers in Lithuania, Poland, and Russia, a Jewish social-democratic movement founded in Vilna in 1897, which fought for the reconstruction of Russia as a democratic state.

4 The Day of Atonement, the most serious Jewish religious holiday, observed on the tenth day of the lunar month of Tishri (in September or October), with a twenty-five-hour fast and extensive prayer.

Judgment, death, and the other world. Aunt Royze did not cry. She kept on letting out a wild hoarse sound like an old angry hen. While this pagan and mystical ceremony was taking place, Uncle Avromke lay on the *piekielnik* (wood stove) shivering badly. This uncanny tableau is still vivid in my mind today.

The second uncle – that is, Grandfather's brother-in-law – who also lived in the shtetl Osmolin was Uncle Mordekhai-Ber. Uncle Mordekhai-Ber was a tall, fit man with a prickly blond beard. His eyes burnt with the cold and sharp fire of a predatory bird. He had strange hands. One hand was missing a finger but had a small mound of reddish flesh, a sign of a finger chopped off. On the other hand, though, he had six complete, healthy fingers. He was illiterate, could not tell a cross from an aleph, and could just barely manage to say the Hebrew benediction on bread. His wife, Grandfather Borukh's sister, Aunt Genendl, was tall and healthy with a big tummy, flaming red face, and a mouthful of sharp white teeth resembling a predatory animal. She had immense prominent breasts like big dangling pots, which always smelt of nursing and of milk. Either she, Aunt Genendl, was nursing and the milk of her breasts was flowing from her unbuttoned blouse, or she was in advanced pregnancy (with Uncle's children). The couple was a personification of sex. When Uncle Mordekhai laughed, it seemed as though thunder rumbled. He also liked to pinch Aunt Genendl's fat and broad behind with his six fingers in front of everybody. They had a whole flock of children. ·

Uncle Mordkhai-Ber had a tavern exactly opposite Uncle Avromke's hovel. Several wooden steps led up to it. There was a constant bad smell of barrels of beer and whisky, of non-kosher sausage and fat roast geese. The whole week long it seemed as though there was no one there. The bottles of liquor and barrels of beer emanated their smell; fat sausages hung on their strings; quiet and fat geese lay on grimy plates. There was quiet in the tavern except for the thundering laughter of Uncle Mordekhai-Ber and the wild shrieks of the nursing or pregnant Aunt Genendl chasing the voracious herd of their children away from the loaded tavern buffet. The true Day of Judgment came on market day, which took place once every week in Osmolin.

Market day in Osmolin is one of the most colourful and beautiful folk events in Poland. Osmolin belonged to the district of Łowicz.[5] The wealthy peasants of the area – the Łowicz soil is among the best in Poland – are famous throughout the land for their decorative and colourful clothing. Even today when one goes through by train on a sunny Sunday in the summer, the eye cannot take in enough of the wonderful romantic splendour of the landscape and the colourful clothing of the peasants bustling around the countryside.

The fields are broken up into a kaleidoscope of varied and vivid colours. The golden ripe wheat, the yellow *łubin*,[6] the white flowers of barley, the green clover, and the meadows – all this plays together in an artistic perspective and in idyllic illumination. The peasants moving about on the roads are dressed in colours matching the colours of the countryside. People there belong to the countryside and blend with it. The Łowicz shawls and coats and the woollen dresses and skirts of the women – it is the countryside around Łowicz that has been woven by the hands and by the dreams of the daughters of the area.

The countryside of Łowicz with the picturesque people moving around evokes the sun colours of Van Gogh. Towards evening, in the fields of Łowicz, when the village church bells toll in the still twilight, the world changes into a symphony of golden sadness, colours, sound, and mood.

The market in Osmolin was especially colourful and reminiscent of the great mass scenes of an opera. Rich peasants in their bright coats came from surrounding villages. The women, healthy and tall, flesh and milk, wore red and green wool dresses, braided ribbons on their arms and in their hair, and were wrapped in the wonderful Łowicz shawls, which reflected the hues of the meadows and fields. On the white and fresh women's necks, bright strings of glass beads. All that whirled in the market in Osmolin amid the carts of well-fed horses, amid tons of juicy plums and fragrant fruit, amid big fat cows, fat woolly rams, and

---

5 A town located sixty kilometres northeast of Łódź.
6 Polish for lupin.

fowl. The market carts on which the Osmoliner Jews stood and traded were full of all kinds of wares, dress material, brightly coloured coats, boots, shawls, and cloth, beads and small holy pictures, blue striped pots, plates, jugs, and cans, tools for work in the field, and in general everything that is necessary for country living. The peasants and the women touched everything, tried on the garments, traded and bargained with the Jews. The Jews sweated, ate and drank in a hurry, also bargained, shouted at the peasant buyers, and helped them try on garments. Pious cripples sang among the unharnessed wagons and on the paving stones. Beggars and the blind murmured prayers and held out their hands. Jewish hurdy-gurdy players played their instruments where green parrots and white field mice drew lots.

The biggest hubbub was in front of Uncle Mordekhai-Ber's tavern. Excited, in trousers and braces, he stood on the wooden steps of the tavern and poured vodka into big glasses. He slapped the drunken peasants on the shoulder. When musicians played and the peasant boys and girls danced, sweating Uncle Mordekhai-Ber with vodka glasses in his hands also took a whirl and danced with the girls. Aunt Genendl, nursing or pregnant, poured liquor into glasses and chased away the peasants who wanted to pinch her behind. During market days the flocks of Uncle Mordekhai-Ber's children besieged the tavern buffet like flies. During market days the children went about dirty and with cheeks covered with grease from their gluttony.

Jews gathered for the prayer *minyan*[7] in Osmolin at Uncle Mordekhai-Ber's. Services were held there on the Sabbath and during the holidays. There, on Simchat Torah, all the Jews of Osmolin got drunk and ate geese and cabbage. A Simchat Torah trustee was elected there. For this great office the biggest *shlimazl*[8] of the Osmolin village community was chosen. The rich men of Osmolin lifted the chosen man as high as the rafters of the synagogue and then let him down hard on the floor. This they did several times in a row until the victim was left on the floor,

---

7 Hebrew: the quorum of ten males required for Jewish prayer.
8 Yiddish for an unlucky person.

dizzy from the great honour. He was also made to drink several full glasses of liquor, and when he was quite drunk, they pulled down his trousers and spanked him.

This was repeated every Simchat Torah. The women also danced and drank and passionately kissed the Torah scrolls. Similar wild spectacles took place on the Ninth of Av.[9] My father told me that during the first Tisha B'Av after his wedding, when he was on his way to recite Lamentations with Uncle Mordekhai-Ber in the *shul*, the following wild scene took place: the rich people of Osmolin were not satisfied with bringing prickly burrs and throwing them in Jewish beards, as was the custom during Lamentations. Instead, immediately after the first verses from the Book of Lamentations were heard, all the oil lamps went out. The synagogue was in pitch darkness. In the darkness, peasant hob-nailed boots began flying around over people's heads. My father only barely managed to hide his head behind a column. He heard shrieks and cries for help in the darkness and the thuds of flying boots. Yells and screams were heard. Suddenly, a woeful cry: My head! A lamp was lit. Gayge's eldest son-in-law, Itshe Motl, lay on the floor in a pool of blood, his head split open. A brawl followed. Simkhe took the belt off his trousers and hit out right and left. Beyla, Simkhe's daughter and Itche's wife, came running and shrieking hysterically for help! 'They have murdered my Itshe Motl.' She set about hitting heads. The synagogue looked like the veritable Destruction of Jerusalem. My father just barely escaped with his life and finished his Lamentations at home.

So much about Uncle Mordekhai-Ber and Aunt Genendl.

One more uncle of mine lived in Osmolin, also a brother-in-law of Grandfather Borukh: Uncle Leyzer Yosef. His wife was Aunt Toybe.

Uncle Leyzer Yosef was an odd type. He was a son of a Jew who farmed land around Sochaczew.[10] As a young boy, he ploughed

---

9 The date in the Jewish calendar on which the Destruction of Jerusalem and the Temple is commemorated and mourned with fasting and lamentations. No drinking or rejoicing occurs on that day, which falls in July or August.

10 A town twenty kilometres northeast of Łowicz.

and harrowed the field together with his father and his brothers. He brought the cattle, cows, and sheep back from grazing in the fields. He never spoke of this, however, and considered himself to be a member of the intelligentsia. Uncle Leyzer Yosef looked down on Uncle Mordekhai-Ber. He tried to speak Polish with a city accent and he habitually read a Polish newspaper. He was a smallish man with the trimmed little beard of an intellectual. Uncle was a bit of a liar and also given to great exaggeration. His lies were not malicious but begotten by his strange whim, produced from his lively imagination. His particular weakness was forever telling about the Turkish-Russian war and about the siege of Pleven.[11]

He was one of Grandfather's 'persons' and always lived near him. As a child, I countless times swallowed his descriptions of the Turkish war, of the drive across the Balkans, and of the siege of Pleven. Uncle's stories inflamed my childish imagination. He told of this war with passion as though he had taken part in it himself. He told of the thundering of the guns on the battlefield, of the attack of the enemy multitude '*na shtiki*,'[12] and of death on the battlefield. He told of soldiers who died lonely, trampled by the stampeding horses, of the chase of the Cossacks, of the struggle with the Turkish cavalry, of the hunger in the besieged fortress, of the fall of Pleven, and of the plunder in the conquered city. Uncle Leyzer Yosef yelled and gesticulated with his hands, just as though he himself had shot, pierced, ridden, and robbed. There will be much more to tell about him in the chapters to follow.

These tales and heroic stories went on as long as he did not fall foul of Aunt Toybe. The moment she gave him a look or, worse, yelled at him, Uncle Leyzer Yosef shrank and became even thinner and smaller than he was. He became pale as a sheet and silent as a mouse, deaf and dumb. He trembled like a fly. He was literally reduced to nothing as soon as she appeared or even

---

11 A Bulgarian town and a famous Turkish stronghold defended heroically by the Turks in 1877 during the Russo-Turkish war.
12 Russian: 'charge bayonets!'

called to him to eat. Aunt Toybe did not have the big bodily amplitude of Aunt Genendl; she was small, thin, her face was green from some pale anger, and she had a very long, sharply delineated nose that stretched over her thin, angrily dry lips. Unlike Aunt Genendl, Aunt Toybe never yelled or cursed. She appeared to be very quiet, but her inner masculine character and the constant bitter anger caused the whole household to go about tremulously whenever her eyes would burn with a reddish fire, her nose lengthened like the beak of a parrot, her lips dried out and shrunk over a small pursed mouth. Uncle Leyzer Yosef would at such a time forget all the battles around Pleven and he would be willing to sink into the ground rather than feel the green glare of Aunt Toybe.

An old and bitter enmity existed between Grandfather Borukh and Aunt Toybe. They never spoke to each other and Grandfather never mentioned her name. Whenever Uncle became inflamed with the fantasy pictures of the war, Grandfather would smile quietly and ironically. He held Uncle in little respect and called him by a nickname, Shoshele.[13]

---

13 A nickname for a little boy.

Chapter Six

In the dense forest Uncle Borukh hears of the prodigy of Kutno. Grand-mother Leah sets out to look the bride over. Disappointment. Reb Yoshua Kutner approves of the engagement. My father and my mother become engaged. Mazel tov.

I purposely lingered over my uncles and aunts in Osmolin in order to convey a sense of the environment in which my mother grew up. The princely 'court' that Grandfather planned to build to honour the wedding of his only daughter did not exist yet. Grandfather still lived with Simkhe Gayge. Simkhe Gayge, his children, his son-in-law, Itshe Motl, and wife, Sore Bine, went barefoot all day long just as all the peasants do. The men ploughed the fields; the daughters milked the cows. The son-in-law, Itshe Motl, who later became a Strykov Hasid and emigrated to America, was still watering the horses in those days and driving wagons into Simkhe's barn. At noon the whole family ate potatoes and borscht, eating with wooden spoons from one big earthen bowl.

Grandfather was in charge of the fertile fields of the Osmólsk estate. His wheat was good and plentiful, and he raised sugar beets for the sugar factory in Sanik. During the snow and cold of the long winter months, Grandfather set out by sleigh into his woods wrapped in a big fearsome bearskin and was away for whole weeks. Grandmother Khaye was then at liberty to deal with all kinds of shady mendicant rabbis and vagabonds and remedies. The only daughter, my mother, grew up with the peasant-like and common family of Simkhe Gayge.

Travelling through the snow in the deep winter woods, the sleighs sounding in the white solitude of frost-covered trees, Grandfather Borukh reflected that his only child, recalled from death by petition, was already approaching marriage age. He should be thinking about a match for her.

Among the lumber clerks whom grandfather employed in his woods were some intelligent Hasidic Jews and learned men. The name of the Kutner prodigy, Reb Yisroel Yoshua Kutner's grand-child, had reached the ears of everyone. It had even travelled as far as the whispering Polish woods. Hereupon it occurred to Grandfather that he would like to have this prodigy as the husband for his little daughter.

Not far from Osmolin, in the shtetl of Gombin,[1] lived an old rabbi, a great *tsadik*, renowned for his simplicity, Reb Moyshe Gombiner. Grandfather went to him and asked him to travel to Kutno and propose the match to R. Yoshua. He was prepared to untie his purse strings and spend a fortune in order to be related to R. Yoshua and have the prodigy for a son-in-law.

Grandfather Moyshl was at the time at the zenith of his depression. Grandmother Leah was a frail woman, an orphan with children. R. Yoshua, as my father used to tell me, suffered from a death complex. Like every rationalist, he had a pessimistic nature. He had an extraordinary sense of the world as an abyss full of evil creatures with death lurking behind every door. R. Yoshua was a pessimist who painted the future in the darkest colours. His often-stated conviction was that after his death the whole family was going to be destitute because his only son was mentally ill and Uncle Yekl was no great shakes as a breadwinner. Bitterly worried, R. Yoshua wanted to save his household from a dark future after he was gone. Therefore the marriage agreement with a rich farmer suited him down to the ground. He saw in it the only practical course for my father.

---

1 A town located twelve kilometres northwest of Sanniki.

As people tell it, when R. Yoshua Kutner saw Grandfather
Borukh Gzhivatsh for the first time, he made a statement that was
really a testing of the waters:

'For a dowry of less than fifteen thousand rubles you will not,
Reb Borukh, have my grandson as a son-in-law' (fifteen thousand
roubles at that time was a fortune). 'However much you want,
Holy Rabbi,' Grandfather answered, 'that I will spend to have you
as kinfolk. My daughter is an only child. Everything will go to her
in any case in a hundred and twenty years. For whom does a
person like me toil day and night? Your grandson will have
nothing more to do in my house than sit amid all the best and
study the Holy Torah.'

Whatever the answer, R. Yoshua was ready to go through with
the match, which he saw as the only resort for my father. The
open-handedness of Grandfather Borukh had impressed him.

It remained for Grandmother Leah to make a trip to see the
bride.

From the start, the noble, suffering, and intelligent Grandmother Leah was not enthusiastic about the marriage. Her oldest
child, my father, was the only radiance in her dark life, a life
allied with a mentally ill husband. Grandmother Leah still lived
at the attic room next to the women's section of the synagogue.
She had pinned her maternal hopes onto this well-turned-out
and greatly loved boy, in whom everything she cherished was
reflected. To give this cosseted child to the peasants in a desolate
village did not sit well with her. R. Yoshua, however, was the only
authority in the family. Grandmother Leah, who grew up among
the Hasids of Praga and Vurke, was used to obeying the commands of *tsadikim.*

But the world went black before Grandmother Leah's eyes
when she entered Simkhe Gayge's place in Osmolin. Simkhe, his
wife, Sore Bine, and the uncles and aunts had no idea how to
treat the well-bred grandchild of a rabbi. They did not know how
to speak quietly and politely, as is the custom in rabbinical courts,
or how to conduct the kind of genteel conversation about the
Torah and Hasidism that Grandmother had known her whole
life. The bride's uncles spoke loudly as the peasants do in the

fields and laughed gustily with their mouths open. These were people of a natural, earthy village life. Peasant Jews. The bride-to-be, my mother, was not one of the pale mollycoddled brides of rabbinical courts. My mother had the easy-going manners of a coarse village background. Grandfather Borukh and Grandmother Khaye didn't even know how to 'gentrify' themselves when they became wealthy. Money was, of course, money, but they knew of no other way of living than that of Osmolin. When Grandmother Leah saw my mother for the first time, she was wearing the common hobnailed shoes that peasant girls in the country wear on Sundays. A welcoming reception in the style of a lease-farmer and with the bride present in heavy peasant shoes made a shocking impression on Grandmother Leah.

On returning to Kutno, she related to R. Yoshua her discomfort in a setting she had never before seen with her own eyes, although she had read about bumpkins and lease-farmers in Yiddish storybooks. Incidentally, my mother never forgot the initial antipathy of Grandmother Leah. R. Yoshua, who was a pessimist by nature and a doomsayer, stuck to his plan. He looked upon the young wife, his daughter-in-law, Grandmother Leah, with her brood of small children, as upon an *agunah*[2] whose husband happened to be alive. What would she do after his, R. Yoshua's, death besides expire from hunger? To care for Grandmother Leah became his only goal.

R. Yoshua contracted the engagement with Grandfather Borukh. My father and mother were engaged. My father was then fourteen years old and my mother was fifteen.

My father was a little, thin, and weak boy.

2 An 'anchored' wife, unable to remarry since her husband has either refused her a divorce or is missing, perhaps dead but without proof.

Chapter Seven

The 'court' in Osmólsk. The journey to Warsaw to buy the bride's trousseau. Simkhe Gayge comes as an expert. Simkhe Gayge in Hekslman's restaurant. Simkhe Gayge in the Warsaw clothing stores. Simkhe Gayge tells the peasants in Osmólsk about the Warsaw wonders. Preparations for the wedding. Grandfather Borukh spares no expense. The jesters. The well-known jester Noah Nashelsker. Fish in the waters of the 'court' of Osmólsk. The family from Osmólsk together with Simkhe Gayge are having silk coats made to measure. Carriages go to Kutno. Uncle Yekl gives advice. Yerakhmiel the butcher in the fields outside the butcher shop in Kutno. Ratse! The 'fool' of the Kutno family. The country uncles try on silk coats. Peasants ride to meet the groom. A welcoming reception for the jesters and Noah Nashelsker. Simkhe Gayge among the rabbis' wives. The country uncles under the apple trees. Reb Yoshua Kutner comes to Osmólsk. Uncle Yekl in the carriage. Hirshl. Hirshl in seven coats and with pockets full of water bottles sits on the coach box. The 'Living Soul,' a wealthy rabbi. Noah Nashelsker recites verses. The ladies' carriage. Yerakhmiel sees surprising things in the fields. Simkhe Gayge takes a shine to Yerakhmiel. Eating in the orchard.

It took fully three years for the great wedding to take place. In the interim my grandfather Moyshl's health returned. This was deemed one of the boons of the union.

The 'court' which Grandfather Borukh built on the Osmólsk estate was now complete. It was a big white house with much light and glass verandas standing in an old overgrown orchard. Behind the 'court' lay a pond surrounded by willows and poplars in which frogs croaked at all times. In front of the house was a big flower bed with roses and lilac bushes. In that 'court' I was born. Grandfather Borukh finally moved out of Simkhe Gayge's house.

After three years, preparations were under way for the wedding. Grandmother Khaye went to Warsaw with the bride-to-be to buy the wedding trousseau. Since Grandmother Khaye was a simple village Jewess without the slightest sense of big-city fashion, Grandmother Leah came along. Grandmother Leah possessed a fine rabbinic taste for female adornment and preferred not to rely on Khaye's taste. She feared what surprises Grandmother Khaye might spring on her and that the bride might not cut the figure of a daughter-in-law of holy *tsadikim* but resemble a village girl in her best Sunday clothes.

Grandfather Borukh sent his faithful Simkhe Gayge to help. I do not know what sage counsel Gayge could have offered about silk crinolines, white dresses worn beneath the wedding canopy, lace, and embroidered woven shirts since he had never before laid eyes on such finery. For years, Gayge talked of this trip with the Kutno rabbi's wife. I remember him doing it. First of all, Gayge felt elevated because of having spent whole days with Grandmother Leah going around the Warsaw shops and dressmakers. Somehow Gayge was included, so it seemed to him, in the requisites of pedigree of the rabbi of Kutno. Secondly, and above all, Gayge could not forget the epic feasts at Hekslman's restaurant in Warsaw, when he filled his stomach with stuffed fish, roast geese and turkeys, rich *tsimmes*,[1] with *kishke*[2] and sweet corn potes. Simkhe Gayge had a peasant stomach accustomed to black bread and potatoes with cabbage. These experiences made an extraordinary impression on him. The man lost his bearings. On returning to Osmolin, he now looked at Grandfather's brothers-

---

1 Carrots, meat, prunes, and honey or sugar cooked together in a stew.
2 Stuffed intestines.

in-law with contempt. He saw them – Mordekhai-Ber, for instance – with new eyes that looked down.

And so preparations began for the great wedding.

For years and years I heard people talk about my parents' wedding. Two families of the Jewish community in Poland came together for the occasion, families that stood at the extremes of Jewish society. On the one side, rabbis, Hasidim, and itinerant preachers and, on the other side, simple and common folk who for generations had lived in the darkling wilds of Polish woods and in the dappled light of Polish fields, Jews who lived together with the Polish peasants and knew little of the noble wisdom of the Torah or of the ways of the urban and middle-class Polish Jews.

Grandfather Borukh spared no expense for the wedding (he was by that time living in the Osmólsk 'court'). He engaged the services of the most famous wedding jesters in Poland, among them that lion of jesters, Noah Nashelsker, to entertain the honoured guests. He also hired two klezmer bands. Chefs and women cooks were sent from Kutno by Grandmother Leah and from Głaznów[3] by Rabbi Engelman, who sent cooks who had prepared the feasts for his weddings. Men specially reared whole flocks of geese, turkeys, and hens. Into the pond behind the 'court' were put big carp, pike, and tench destined for the plates of the *tsadikim* invited to the wedding. They ate and grew even bigger in the hot summer waters. The water in the pond teemed with fish. Frogs croaked happily in the muddy rushes at the edges of the pond. They too ate of the peas and lupin thrown in for the fish.

In addition to ordering a rich trousseau for the bride, my grandfather also ordered new clothes for himself and Grand-mother Khaye in order to gain status in the eyes of the esteemed relatives. The uncles and the aunts also decked themselves out in city clothes for the wedding. Simkhe Gayge spent days telling the peasants of his camaraderie with Grandmother Leah, of the

---

3 A village fifteen kilometres west of Kutno.

velvets and silks in the shops of Warsaw, and of the food in Hek-slman's restaurant. Simkhe, too, had a long Hasidic silk coat made for the first time in his life.

Everybody felt that a new era of pride had arrived for Grand-father's entire tribe in Osmolin.

Just before the wedding, Grandfather Borukh borrowed car-riages from all the landed gentry in the area and their most elegant black horses as well. He sent them to Kutno to convey the guests, Reb Yoshua Kutner, and the bridegroom. He also sent his personal carriage, which he had bought because of the new era. Kutno was jammed with the carriages of the nobility. The Jews of Kutno thronged the lanes near the house of the rabbi, staring at the opulence. The pure-blooded black horses proudly neighed in front of Reb Yoshua's courtroom. Coachmen dressed to the nines in livery and sporting long moustaches stood near the study house and cracked their whips. The noblemen's servants were somewhat inebriated from the ample bottles of liquor that Grandfather Borukh had distributed for the road.

The Jews of Kutno long afterwards remembered the train of carriages awaiting the wedding guests. Uncle Yekl made the biggest stir. Although standing at a distance on the steps of the study house and fearful of the slightly drunk Christian drivers with their whips, he imparted advice to them anyway. He gave various tips about driving out of Kutno. He thought, of course, that one would do best to take to the road at three in the morning, sleep in one's clothes in the carriage, and have a quick meal in the woods.

Uncle Yekl had a son-in-law of his own whose name was Yer-akhmiel. Yerakhmiel was tall and blond and had a blond goatee. Everybody called him a fool. He admitted as much himself and was in the habit of saying: 'Listen, what do I know. I'm a fool.' His wife, Ratse, Uncle Yekl's daughter, was small, pale, and sickly with an uncommonly long chin and the screechy voice of an angry turkey. Every time Yerakhmiel opened his mouth, Ratse said in her tiny voice, 'Quiet, Yerakhmiel, sweetheart. A fool doesn't mix in when people are talking.' Yerakhmiel tugged on his goatee beard and lowered his head, exactly as if to declare, 'You're right,

Ratse. A fool doesn't mix in.' When he was in a mood sometimes to comment on or even to chime in with one of Uncle Yekl's 'tips,' the latter would cut him short at once and say, 'Quiet. You're a fool!'

There will be much more about Uncle Yerakhmiel later, and I am only writing about him now because the only thing that he had a licence to converse about and that he indeed did converse about whenever he could, in full measure and in detail, was the theme of the carriages and the baronial splendour that Grandfather Borukh lavished far and wide in honour of the great wedding.

Many, many years later, when Yerakhmiel was sick and broken, an invalid with hernias on both sides of his body and the declared fool of the whole family, his spent and sickly eyes would glint in sweet reminiscence. The goatee on his chin would bristle upwards. Even his wife, Ratse, and his father-in-law, Uncle Yankel, who never let him utter a word and constantly reminded him that a fool stays quiet, even they, the guardians of his foolishness, were still and smiled complacently and allowed him to be effusive in recalling his only glory, that is, my father's wedding. Yerakhmiel, who was in no rush, told and retold it with all the details.

In the meantime, at the court in Osmólsk, preparations were afoot for the wedding. As I've already written, Grandfather Borukh had brand new silk *kapotes*[4] made at his expense for the brothers-in-law, Uncle Mordekhai-Ber and Uncle Leyzer Yosef, and for his brother, Uncle Avromke. The idea was that the country uncles should be more presentable to the Hasidic rebbes and the rabbis at the wedding. Uncle Leyzer Yosef, who constantly fantasized about the Turkish-Russian war and who read a Polish newspaper, felt that the silk coat became him and befitted him as a member of the intelligentsia. All of a sudden on the Wednesday before the wedding, he tried on the spanking-new crisp coat and stood in the middle of the room erupting into a cantorial aria. He liked to lead in services at the rostrum. In addi-

---

4 A traditional long gabardine man's coat worn by Jews.

tion to everything else, he thought he had a musical bent. Angry and green-complexioned Aunt Toybe just then came into the room carrying a pot of sour milk and saw something she had not seen before: Uncle Leyzer Yosef standing by himself in the long Hasidic silk coat in the middle of the room, loudly quavering. Her complexion became still greener, and she plunked down the pot of sour milk and began to shower him with expletives, which instantly caused him to become shorter by two heads and abruptly to take off the silk coat and crawl into the coop among the chickens. Aunt Toybe yelled for a long time more in her squeaky voice, and Uncle Leyzer Yosef trembled among the chickens like a leaf. Grandfather's brother, Uncle Avromke, also was given a long silk coat. He looked it at with reverence and was scared to put his hands on it, as a simple Jew is awe-stricken by an *etrog*.[5] Aunt Royze in her Turkish shawl and the bird on her cap persisted in asking Uncle Avromke just to try the coat on for size before the wedding. As a matter of curiosity, she wanted to see what the old boy would look like in grand and spiffy attire. It was no good. Uncle Avromke broke out in trembling and would not touch the silk coat except to lay it on his bed. He stood looking at it with profound homage. In contrast, Uncle Mordekhai-Ber looked elegant when he wore the coat once on a Sunday. He stood on the steps of the tavern and loudly called to the peasants, who almost did not recognize him dressed up like a Hasidic Jew. Aunt Genendl was very pregnant and stood next to him chewing on a piece of bread and butter. Uncle Mordekhai-Ber burst out laughing at the top of his voice, standing on the steps, and jovially, with all six fingers, gave her a good pinch on the behind. The innumerable throng of his children fluttered around the laden buffet, snatching whatever food they could.

Not long before the arrival of the carriages with the wedding-guests, Grandfather enjoined the uncles to, for God's sake, keep their distance and not to make a scene of themselves before the

---

5 Hebrew: 'citron,' one of four plants used during the celebration of Sukkot (Feast of Booths). The *etrog* is traditionally very expensive and potentially fragile.

eyes of the distinguished guests, notwithstanding that they were wearing silk Hasidic coats.

The sound of drivers' trumpets was heard.

Grandfather's farmhands rode out on well-appointed horses to meet them. The horses were adorned with leafy branches and colourful Łowicz trappings and ribbons. It was the month of Tamuz (June–July). The Jewish klezmer bands which Grandfather had mustered from the neighbouring towns played the 'Blessed be he who cometh' melody. Wearing big velvet skullcaps, the jesters, including the chief jester, Noah Nashelsker, stood in a reception line in order to greet the important guests with Yiddish verses and Hebrew wedding songs specially composed for the occasion. The rattle of wheels on the road and the blare of the trumpets got louder. The trumpets obstreperously clashed with one another. The women, even the mother of the bride, Grandmother Khaye, the bride, Aunt Royze in her Turkish shawl, and the other women in the family, made themselves scarce in the rooms of the 'court' so their feminine presence would not obstruct the grand entrances of the Gaon Yoshua Kutner, of the Hasidic rebbes, and of the other well-known rabbis who had come to honour the Kutner. Behind the white curtains at the windows the women looked out onto the porch to see the arrival of the bridegroom's distinguished relatives.

Grandfather Borukh Gzhivatsh had put on his long black Sabbath coat and stood among the jesters.

Simkhe Gayge fancied himself to be somewhat a member of the 'other side.' For had he not gone round the Warsaw dry goods shops with Grandmother Leah to buy silks for the bride and even accompanied her to the well-known dressmaker who sewed dresses for rich Warsaw ladies? He, Simkhe Gayge, had also somewhere procured his own long black coat, in which he looked like the effigy of a rebbe at a village Purim party. Wearing the coat, he darted among the tables bearing vodka, wines, and cakes, which had been put out amid the flower beds in front of the house for the arriving wedding guests to have a first bite. Simkhe Gayge wore (for the first time in his life) a velvet skullcap. Perspiring heavily, he chased away gawking village peasant girls by shooing them off with gross obscenities while he chewed a chunk of cake with big smacks.

The three uncles, Uncle Avromke, Uncle Mordekhai-Ber, and Uncle Leyzer Yosef, who were forbidden by Grandfather to be conspicuous around the honoured relatives, stood separately under three ripe apple trees and looked on stealthily. All three had the new long silk coats on. Uncle Avromke stood alone, bowed and cringing, his eyes lowered to the grass. Pregnant Aunt Genendl stood with Uncle Mordekhai-Ber. Uncle Mordekhai was also wearing a big velvet skullcap and his black silk coat was unbuttoned and wide open over his sumptuous and protuberant belly. Terrified Aunt Genendl held him by the hand. His burning eyes sparkled like the eyes of a lurking wolf from behind the apple tree. With six fingers, he shook off Aunt Genendl, who clung to him ever tighter as if she wanted protection from the eeriness of the arriving rabbis. Uncle Leyzer Yosef with Aunt Toybe also stood behind an apple tree. He alone of the uncles was sick at heart that Grandfather forbade him to mix freely with the honoured guests. Uncle Leyzer Yosef held himself to be a 'cut above' the other uncles. Didn't he read a Polish newspaper, talk about the Turkish war, and love to lead synagogue services? Galling him the most was that such a one as Simkhe Gayge had the freedom of the house among the musicians and the jesters and the tables with all manner of goodies on them, and would probably be one of the first to get to the Kutner rabbi by pushing with his big peasant paws and extend to him a broad hello. Such a yokel! For everything in the world, one needs to have luck, and the devil only knows why Simkhe Gayge was the one who went to Warsaw with Grandmother Khaye and the bride-to-be and who got into an in-law-like rapport with the bride's future mother-in-law, the daughter-in-law of the Kutner. Simkhe Gayge was now an authority on silk garments and had partaken of the fish and meat of Warsaw at Hekslman's restaurant. (Simkhe had not stopped dazzling the peasants with this story. When he told it in the market, he peppered it with racy phrases and curses.) It happened that Uncle Leyzer Yosef felt entirely at home in the silk Hasidic coat. He repeatedly slid out from behind the apple tree

with the object of gaining the guests' attention, but angry Aunt
Toybe, experienced, caught his arm each time and delivered such
invective that it made Uncle Leyzer Yosef shrivel in his silk coat
and become quiet and helpless as a child.

The carriages had in the meantime driven up to the 'court'
and the drivers halted the overheated horses.

The bands of musicians played louder and the jesters began
their quips. The commanding voice of the famous Noah Nashelsker was heard.

Rabbi Yoshua Kutner descended from the first coach wearing a
large silk coat lined with fur and a sable hat. After him emerged
his son, Grandfather Moyshl, with the darkly charming bridegroom.

Uncle Yekl had elbowed himself into the carriage for the ride
even though travelling with Rabbi Yoshua was not his idea of fun.
First of all, Rabbi Yoshua studied the whole way and had a sharp
Torah discussion with the bridegroom. The sharpest insights,
challenges, and retorts flew from the Kutner's mouth as swift as
arrows from a bow. To appreciate their sharp Talmudic ideas, you
had to know the Talmud and know Rabbi Yoshua's quirks of
expression. My father was always with his erudite grandfather and
learned his lessons from him, so he had no problem in understanding him. Besides, my father was a genius and the future
'second Kutner.' But the trip was noxious for Uncle Yekl. His
tastes ran to a strong shot of liquor or a Hasidic celebration in a
synagogue or a card game with Hasidim or a common Yiddish
word from Vurke. As I have already written, the Kutner mostly
ignored Yekl, barely speaking to him at all. It must have been
pure misery for Uncle Yekl to travel cheek by jowl with the genius
in the same a carriage, in such a high-tension Torah mood, but
he dug in anyway and went all the way with them! For Uncle Yekl
was by nature deeply curious, curious as a child about everything
and everybody. He was curious to know what a wedding in a baronial 'court' would look like. It was said that the bride's father had
millions of rubles, an esoteric concept to Uncle Yekl. He imagined sumptuous plates descending from the skies to tender
service to the wedding guests, and he wanted to be the first to see

what heavenly dishes looked like and how guests ate chicken soup in which gold coins floated. He had heard much about the assembled bands of musicians and the famous jesters who would appear with their songs and sayings. Besides, Uncle Yekl was a great one for ecstatic raptures and klezmer music, and he swooned at the high comedic turns of a jester. That the bride's family were country people who barely knew the Hebrew alphabet did not concern him. First of all, he had meagre affinity with learning himself. Learning had brought him nothing but headache and unhappiness and ostracism. Secondly, he was full of Hasidic love for the Jewish people. A cheerful, ordinary Jew was closer to his heart than the lauded and mostly bewildering men of learning. Uncle Yekl was a true Vurker Hasid, without airs or tricks, one of the people. He was a man of warm heart and an uncomplicated allegiance to Judaism with an infantile curiosity.

Together with R. Yoshua and some of the wedding guests, the attendant Hirshl climbed heavily down from the coach box. Hirshl had sat there alongside the mustachioed Gentile driver. Hirshl had held tight to his pockets, believing that doing so would prevent him from falling off the carriage, for the Gentile driver drove the horses at a fast gallop. All the pockets of the seven coats that Hirshl wore on top of each other in spite of the summer heat were crammed with full bottles of water. Hirshl carried these water bottles all the way from Kutno so that R. Yoshua could wash his hands along the way.

Hirshl (or Hirshl the Trustee) was a tall, heavy man with a moulting beard, a pretty sizable rich man's pot belly and was blind in one eye. He had two sources of income. One was as a supervisor in the Kutno butcher shops dealing with butchers who were deathly afraid of him. His seven long coats were smeared with blood and grease, and one could smell from them a stale and ugly odour of flesh, which could be detected a mile away. His second income came from service as R. Yoshua's chief attendant. His tasks were lighting R. Yoshua's pipe, bringing slaughtered geese to Grandmother Prive, and collecting money from rich Jews who wished an audience with R. Yoshua. Hirshl was a cheerful kind of a guy who was always smiling with the one eye left in his full face. Despite reeking of a sour, ugly smell of flesh and the slaughterhouse, he thrust himself everywhere and loved the company of the Vurke Hasidim. He considered himself to be a terrific Hasidic dancer. On Purim and on Simchat Torah he kept pace with Uncle Yekl, blackening his face with soot and dancing in the middle of the street in his seven stinking coats and singing at the top of his squeaky, hoarse voice. All his days his home life was bitter and gloomy. His wife was crazy since her first pregnancy. Merry and half-blind Hirshl had to spend his life with a crazy wife. She ripped her clothes off, threw her feathered bonnet off her shaven head, and standing half-naked, beat Hirshl with a broom and threw pots at him. Hirshl often had to flee his home as though it was on fire, and the neighbours on occasion suffered from insomnia because of the shrieks of the crazy woman, but Hirshl remained self-confident and energetic and took out his anger on the slaughtered oxen and on the butchers. His wife's condition did not prevent him from having a goodly number of children with her, big strong sons who left the path of righteousness and got mixed up with the Kutno underworld and a string of healthy daughters with burning, sickly eyes who were black as the purest gypsies. He brought husbands for the girls, yeshiva students from neighbouring small towns, and subsidized their Torah study, allowing the couples to live in his house with him and his crazy wife. The dark daughters teemed with children, and Hirshl's home became a real nightmare.

To travel in a coach was one of Hirshl's greatest sensual pleasures. Whenever R. Yoshua needed to go to a nearby shtetl to adjudicate or to quiet a controversy over a rabbi, perhaps about whether an old-timer with questionable ordination should be allowed to recite the nuptial blessings, or to confer with another authority, Hirshl – as the accompanying attendant – could be relied upon to find a reason why R. Yoshua should get there by coach. Hirshl, also a Vurker Hasid, constantly quarrelled with Uncle Yekl, mainly about issues connected with the coach. Although nobody asked him or listened to his advice, Uncle Yekl always proffered an opinion about the best route for R. Yoshua's forays. A perverse and convoluted opinion it goes without saying.

When the longed-for coach pulled up to the building that housed R. Yoshua's courtroom, Hirshl at once clambered onto the coachman's box. The pockets of his seven coats contained bottles filled with water. He would wait for an hour for R. Yoshuale to appear, and all that time he quarrelled with Uncle Yekl. Uncle Yekl stood on the steps of the court looking with envy at Hirshl. Uncle Yekl never travelled with R. Yoshua, never except for my father's wedding.

Climbing down from the second coach that stopped at the 'court' was the famous rabbi of Kalisz, the renowned author of *The Living Soul.* The Kalisher's celebrity in Poland did not rest on his learning so much as on his, as it was, impressive worldliness. The competence of the great rabbis of Poland did not go beyond the province of Jewish law. They were not worldly-wise and did not know the dictates of fashion. They lived modestly as paupers or as *kheyder* teachers. The Kalisher kept a rich man's establishment. He came from a wealthy family in Austria and married (the first time) a rich man's daughter, also from Austria. He carried a sense of rabbinical worldliness with him when he entered the dowdy and poor atmosphere of Polish rabbis and Hasidic rebbes, which was tremendously impressive. He even allowed his daughters to attend a secular school where they learned German and Polish and read Schiller and Mickiewicz.[6] These cultivated and proud daughters acted more like ladies than rabbinic daughters, having nothing in common with such a dowdy Jewish woman as the pious Aunt Sorel. The rabbi of Kalisz had arranged the marriages of the wealthiest Hasidim in Poland, such as Reb Yeshaya Prywes, Reb Yekl Engelman, and Reb Itshe Blas. I'll have more to tell about these people later.

The Kalisher rabbi dwelled in sumptuous rooms and behaved more like a rich man than like a rabbi. He even had a flower garden next to the house and every morning went out in the garden to tie up the beautiful and exquisite roses he grew. This was exotic behaviour for a Polish rabbi. He had the aura of a

---

6 Adam Mickiewicz (1798–1855), one of the greatest Polish poets and national sages.

Jewish prince. He was also devoted to the Jewish community in the land of Israel as that concept was understood in those days. He intensely wanted to reform the beggarly Halukah[7] distribution of alms from the Diaspora. He found a certain Warsaw Jew, a patron, and persuaded him to build houses in Jerusalem. The houses, for which the Kalisher had vague construction plans, ultimately fell to the Halukah. The Kalisher rabbi had more modern plans for the settlements of the Land of Israel than did the impractical Polish rabbis. He supported the Jewish agricultural colonies that were beginning to be founded in the Land of Israel. In Poland itself he led a strong campaign for Jews exclusively to buy *etrogim* (citrons) from the Land of Israel. The Polish rabbis had some qualms about these *etrogim*. They were of the opinion that *etrogim* from Corfu were comelier and more kosher and worthier of the holy blessing. Taking a particular dislike to the Land of Israel *etrogim* were the Hasidic rabbi of Ger,[8] later author of *The Language of Truth (Sefat-Emet)*, and the well-known controversialist, the Radzyner rebbe, R. Gershon Henekh.

Interestingly, this same Gershon Henekh discovered the hillazon, or snail fish, and agitated intensely for Jews to start wearing *tekhelet* or blue fringes (*tsitsis*).[9] However, the polemical and aggressive style in which the Radzyner rabbi spoke publicly harmed the hillazon cause. Polish Hasidic rebbes came out against the blue *tsitsis* reform, and no one except Radzyner Hassidim wore them and are still wearing them today. The same Rabbi Gershon Henekh led a bitter fight against the Kalisher rabbi and his Land of Israel citrons. The Kalisher rabbi defended the citrons in a large responsum published at the beginning of his book *The*

---

7 The distribution of charitable donations from Jews in the Diaspora to individual Jews and various Jewish institutions in Palestine.

8 Ger – in Polish, Góra Kalwaria (Mount of Calvary) – a small town just south of Warsaw, was an important centre of the Hasidic movement and the headquarters of the Gerer rebbe. The first Gerer was Itskhok Meir Alter (1785–1866), who established the dynasty. Yehuda Aryeh Leib Alter (1847–1905), the Gerer rebbe from 1870, published his collected works as *Sefat-Emet* (1905–8).

9 The Torah specifies inclusion of a blue thread in the fringes required on the rectangular garment. See Numbers 15: 37–41 and commentaries thereon.

Living Soul. Since the Radzyner rabbi was not able to debate except in a ferocious and insulting manner, the purely theoretical dispute presently turned into deadly enmity. The Radzyner rabbi deployed ugly personal attacks in his campaign against the Kalisher rabbi. He tore into his salons and his roses, saying that these objects of wealth imitated Gentile ways. He charged that the daughters of the Kalisher rabbi studied foreign languages and, as the *coup de grâce,* that Gentile servants were employed in his house. Opposing non-Jewish servants was the Radzyner rabbi's chief charge, and he wrote a long responsum in a very polemical tone with nasty attacks on the Kalisher rabbi. Things went so far that the second wife of the rabbi of Kalisz, the status-conscious Aunt Shifra-Mirele, once went to her father with the complaint that he, Rabbi Yoshua, should no longer let the Radzyner rabbi into the house (as I will describe later in more detail, the rabbi of Radzyn used often to visit Reb Yoshua). The sedate and patrician rabbi of Kalisz had, in the end, to leave Kalisz for the following reason: as Kalisz was a frontier town with Germany, many rich progressive Jews, the so-called 'Germans,' lived there. Winds from Berlin began to blow and the 'Germans' wanted to reform the *shul,* that is, to move the reading desk directly in front of the Holy Ark (away from the traditional middle position). The Kalisher rabbi reacted belligerently. The outcome was that the 'German' reformers turned to the tried-and-true means with which disputes were resolved in those days: they denounced the Kalisher rabbi to the Russian governor. The 'Living Soul' had to leave Kalisz. He left for Warsaw. He was well-known for his worldliness, and the wealthiest Jews of Warsaw took their litigation and disputes to him. In Warsaw, too, he lived in sumptuous rooms and in style. Later he became the rabbi of Piotrków.[10]

But let me return to the approaching carriages.

Other important wedding guests meanwhile descended from the other carriages. Yerakhmiel, Uncle Yekl's son-in-law, sat on the coachman's box together with a Gentile. He could not marvel

---

10 A large town located forty kilometres south of Łódź.

enough at the many wonders that he beheld during the fabulous journey. All that Yerakhmiel saw from the first minute when he sat down in the carriage in Kutno until the seven nuptial benedictions were recited made the deepest impression on him and awoke the secret conviction that remained with him for the rest of his years that this wedding was the only heroic and bright spot in his life, a life that he spent in fear of Aunt Ratse and under the thumb of his father-in-law, Uncle Yekl. Uncle Yekl habitually crowned him the fool and *shlimazl* of the family, although, as regards haplessness, Uncle Yekl himself was surely the greater ne'er-do-well. For Yerakhmiel ended up as the ritual slaughterer of Kutno. He cultivated a huge bloody nail on his hand, used to test his shiny knives. When Yerakhmiel, I still remember it, appeared in the streets of Kutno with these dazzling knives and his blood-spattered goatee, one might think that this was a younger cousin of the Angel of Death himself if it weren't that this Jewish assassin always walked piteously bent over and wore his hundred frailties on his sleeve and, above all, became pale as chalk and sprang into flight whenever the smallest dog appeared. Because he held his sickly and emaciated wife, Ratse, to be a great authority, Yerakhmiel, who had slaughtered the biggest oxen, trembled in her presence like a fish in water. As soon as he saw a dog, he would reflexively shriek at the top of his voice, Ratse! Even when she was not within earshot of his cries, he would still cry for her when there was a little dog in the fields outside the slaughterhouse, from which were heard the roars of the fat oxen awaiting Yerakhmiel's knife. Yerakhmiel of the bloody goatee and glinting knives would yell, Ratse!

Back to the carriages.

Next came the carriages with the important female wedding guests. From the first coach emerged Grandmother Prive with the Kalisz *rebetsn*. The latter excelled in her big-city attire, as she held the old and rather provincial Grandmother Prive by the hand and hardly looked at anybody else, not at the klezmer bands and not at the singing jesters, not even at the famous Noah Nashelsker, who in the midst of the tumult sang and spoke in his lion's voice wonderful quips that were not coarse and plebeian at all, as were those of the lesser jesters. Noah's jesting was pervaded and threaded with an artful combination of Talmud and Midrashic legends and peppered with mystical letter analyses of *notarikon* and *gematria*,[11] each of which contained the names of the bride and groom and of their sainted parents. The daughter of the Kutner and the wife of the Kalisher rabbi, who now lived in a magnificent apartment in Warsaw and who ate honey cake and butter cookies every day and socialized with the wealthiest women in Warsaw, she, the wife of the Kalisher, used as she was to the rational sphere of analysis and erudition, had enormous contempt for feminine nonsense devised for women and common men. On the other hand, the real honoured lady on the bridegroom's side, his mother, Grandmother Leah, who emerged third from the carriage after the *rebetsn* of Kalisz, was a great admirer of klezmer and jesters' pieces. She was used to rhyming from her Vurker times. The Young Vurker himself rhymed in Yiddish. Also Leah's mother, Grandmother Blimele, loved composing rhymes in common Yiddish.

In the second women's coach sat the pious Aunt Sorel, Uncle Yekl's wife, with her daughters. Ratse jumped out first from the coach and looked around for Yerakhmiel, who was at the same time clambering down from the coachman's box with all his hundred frailties. His face burned from the wonders, and his yellow goatee stood up on his chin. He wondered at everything and everybody, at the peasants who stood off at a distance in their colourful Łowicz jackets, at the fruit trees laden with luscious fruit, which Yerakhmiel had only seen before in baskets at the Kutno fair. And here they grew wild on trees belonging to the Jewish landowner. So many boisterous klezmer bands and singing jesters. And tables with an assortment of good things. Honey cakes and liquor and wine! Never had Yerakhmiel beheld anything like this before. A millionaire's profusion, may it not attract the evil eye. His head was still full of another wonder, namely, that in the fields crossed by the carriage he saw many

---

11 Kabbalistic methods of text analysis.

oxen and cows grazing in droves or ploughing the earth. Yerakhmiel was used to animals lying bound in the slaughterhouses.
He was used to reciting blessings over them and then dispatch-
ing them with his shiny knives. The world is full of sights and
wonders indeed. Yerakhmiel even found favour in the eyes of
Simkhe Gayge, who, perspiring in the long black silk coat and
tall black velvet yarmulke, bustled amidst the tables piled with
delicacies, amidst the rabbis, and yelled at the peasants and
shooed away the peasant girls. Simkhe Gayge had clawed
gobbets of honey cake for himself and did not forget to chew the
big pieces. The hapless Yerakhmiel, a stranger in these parts,
stood in the midst of the wedding turmoil, his yellow goatee
trembling, out of place looking for Ratse. He fell into Simkhe
Gayge's line of vision: 'He looks to be among the elite guests but
he's a quiet, harmless little man who will let you talk to him.'
And so Simkhe put a piece of cake into Yerakhmiel's mouth.
Poor Yerakhmiel just bit into it with great fear and ineptness and
only managed to yell 'Ratse!' The healthy and excited Simkhe
Gayge gave him a brotherly slap on the back, as is the peasant
fashion, and robustly dragged him to the tables with the goodies
on them. A short peasant who was standing in the way received
a kick in the rear with the hobnailed boot and a loud and gross
peasant curse. Poor Yerakhmiel groaned 'Ratse!' but it helped
him as much as cupping helps a corpse. He was in Simkhe
Gayge's hands.

   In the meantime the important guests were being received.
Grandfather Borukh pushed his way to R. Yoshua Kutner and the
bridegroom and with deep servility said to them: '*Sholem-Aleykhem*'
and then repeated it to the rabbi of Kalisz. He led them towards
the set tables and seated R. Yoshua Kutner and the 'Living Soul'
at the head table. The groom sat in the middle between the two
world-famous scholars. One by one the other wedding guests also
took their places at the tables. All waited until R. Yoshua opened
the festivities. When he bit into the first slice of cake, the hungry
guests dived in. Uncle Yekl had in the meantime quarrelled with
the attendant Hirshl, who smelled of the butcher shop even in

the middle of the orchard. Water was pouring from Hirshl's pockets, for the bottles in his seven coat pockets had popped open in honour of the great joyous occasion, and water spouted from Hirshl as though from a fountain. Uncle Yekl was giving advice, but in the great commotion nobody heard it. He found his son-in-law Yerakhmiel at last and sat down with him at the table. Everybody relaxed on the lawn in front of the 'court' and ate honey cake and toasted '*l'chaim*' to the distinguished rabbis and to the groom. Only the country uncles in their silk coats stood under the apple trees and dared not approach the tables with the important relatives.

In the meantime, Grandmother Khaye with the bride came out to greet the female guests. There Simkhe Gayge was active. Considering himself a good friend, he kept near Grandmother Leah. He laughed and shrieked at the top of his thick voice and led the female wedding guests to Grandmother Khaye and the bride, who stood shyly on the steps of the porch and looked on. The rabbis' wives and women of Kutno came closer. They were led to the set tables standing on the other side of the 'court,' far from the men. There too a band of klezmorim was playing. At the head of the table were seated Grandmother Prive and the wife of the Kalisher rabbi. Between them sat the none-too-confident bride. For the first time in her life, she sat near rabbis' wives. Here too wine and honey cake was served, only instead of bottles of common liquor, carafes were set out with coloured, sweet feminine liqueurs.

Simkhe Gayger, the tall velvet yarmulke on his head and his long black coat unbuttoned, fussed at the women's tables, exchanged greetings and wishes at the top of his thick peasant voice with the other rabbis' wives, and urged the bride on, telling her not to be shy. Among the important women, he felt uplifted to seventh heaven and gave not a glance towards the country uncles standing far away in their new long black coats as if they were strangers in these parts. When they were all fortified, all the relatives, the rabbis, and their wives stood up from the tables. They were led to prepared rooms that they might lie down and rest after the long journey in preparation for the great wedding tomorrow.

Uncle Yekl was busy with his son-in-law, Yerakhmiel, and loudly calling him a fool in everybody's hearing.

All the klezmer bands stopped playing and it became quiet.

Chapter Eight

Wagons of Jewish poor people on the Polish roads. Inside the wagons, behind the stove in study houses and in the shelters for the homeless, poor people tell tales about R. Yoshua Kutner. Jewish poor people among village Jews. Jewish poor people in Grandmother Khaye's kitchen. The poor women bless Sabbath candles in the fields. In beggars' carts there is talk about the preparations going ahead for my parents' wedding. Grandfather Borukh orders the barn and orchard laid open to the poor. The meal for the poor.

Both during those days and continuing on into the years of my youth, Jewish beggars of Poland were divided into two classes. First, there were the entrenched town beggars, consisting of male beggars and all manner of female beggars, young and old. They lived among the Jewish underworld in poor back alleys alongside hurdy-gurdy men, jugglers, thieves, and 'merry houses.' In their habitat of back alleys the professional beggars didn't seem so desolate and friendless. Friday was a begging day, and all the beggars surfaced. They made a point of dressing in tattered clothes and displaying piteous bodily deformities to arouse compassion. On Friday various imitation and phoney cripples came out in force, cripples with bandaged necks and faces and hands, cripples on crutches, and beggarly cripples who crawled on the ground. The women made themselves look old, ugly, and frail. Working en masse, they engulfed the Jewish houses and shops. They did not beg but, standing still and morose, demanded pennies. And woe to anyone who tried to refuse! They howled and swore. Eerie curses reminiscent of the world beyond echoed from the mouths in the bandaged faces of the dirty and ragged beggars.

However, there was in Poland another sort of Jewish beggar. These were the beggars wandering over the fields and villages of Jewish communities. These were the so-called mendicant Jewish country walkers. Country wanderers. Mendele Moykher-Sforim[1] in *Fishke the Lame* describes such itinerant Jewish poor of Volhynia.[2] But they existed in Poland too and lived like Gypsies, although they made no copper kettles, stole no horses, did not lay out cards to read fortunes, did not have tribal kings, did not live in wagons in the Polish woods or in open harvest fields next to Polish villages. The Jewish beggars also trudged from one village to another in dilapidated cloth-covered wagons harnessed to sick, crippled, and half-blind horses. The carts, packed with whole families of the wandering poor, barely made it over the Polish roads. The people slowly lumbered from village to village, stopping over at night with Jewish dairymen and saloon keepers and inside barns and on haystacks. They hung about cowsheds, among the cows, and begged from the village Jews for a little milk and freshly baked country bread. On Sabbaths they descended on the wealthier farmers. If a Jewish farmer-landowner lived somewhere in a neighbourhood, they arrived by Thursday dusk (in summer mostly, for in the snowy winters Jewish beggars as good as disappeared from the Polish roads). They waited out the cold months in poorhouses which were found hard by the graveyards of the Jewish towns. The cloth-covered carts carrying poor Jews moved in every direction. Once on the landowner's grounds, they spread out around the stables and the grain piles and haystacks. As a rule, these poor people were profoundly silent. Their ragged clothes reeked of the fields

---

1 A pen name of Sholem Abramovitsh (1835–1917), one of the most outstanding Yiddish writers, considered the 'grandfather' of modern Yiddish literature.
2 A region located south of the Pripet Marshes and east of the River Bug, today in northwestern Ukraine.

and of the sun. Women and girls were not in the gangs that approached village Jews but were busy somewhere with cooking and women's chores. Only the men begged from the village Jews. The hordes also contained grotesque cripples, the lame, the deformed, the blind, and people who were covered with boils. The cripples worked hard in the stables and barns, raking up bits of rotting hay that were lodged in sand or under stones near the barn. They pulled up grass in the ditches – for fodder for their emaciated, bloodshot-eyed and dirty-eyed and neglected horses. The mendicant horses, humble-hearted and servile, stood tied to the linen-covered carts and waved their tails to shake off the flies and gnats that had alighted on their scaly hides to suck blood.

Even in the years of my youth the big kitchen at the 'court' was full of those ragged, laconic paupers. They carried sacks and dark earthenware pots and begged for milk and bread. Grandmother Khaye had big pots on the blazing hearth to make gruel borscht for the poor Jews who had come to the door. The maids and the Gentile girls working for my grandfather in the kitchen poured out full bowls for them. Big slabs of bread were cut, thickly spread with butter and cheese. The poor Jews chewed the bread and drank the borscht silently. They did not give thanks or make any kind of statement. They darkly muttered into their wild, unkempt beards, said a blessing before eating, or quickly said their blessings afterwards. Then they put the bread into their bags and poured the milk that Grandmother Khaye had given them into their earthenware pots and departed soundlessly.

The lights that one saw in the fields on Friday evening were penny candles that the beggars' wives had lit for the Sabbath.

On Friday evening the poor came to pray. They silently waited near the door of the synagogue. The village *shul* filled with the smell of their coats, which was the smell of sun and field. I never saw them look into the prayer book or actually pray. They were quiet as mutes. Later on they were taken into the kitchen and given big bread slices and fish sauce. They dipped the bread in the fish sauce and loudly chewed the bones of the meat they were given and then silently took their leave and disappeared in the darkness of the rustling orchard.

When there was a wedding at a Jewish landowner's estate, word of it was spread throughout the whole of Poland by the travelling beggar wagons, that is, that such and such a Jewish landowner was making a wedding. The cloth-covered wagons were drawn to the wedding from nearly all over Poland.

The announcement of my parents' wedding spread like wildfire among the wagons because it was more than just a wealthy Hasid's wedding. A millionaire Jewish farmer was marrying his little daughter, his only child, to the grandson of Rabbi Yoshua Kutner. The greatest rabbis and holy men of Poland will be there. The millionaire farmer is sparing no expense. Poor people who had lately drifted through the Osmólsk estate spun sensational stories in barns and haystacks all over the country about the armies of chicken, geese, and turkeys that were being reared for the wedding. About the estate waters thick with carp and pike that are being fed nutriments to fatten them and make them fit for a king. And of the barrels of wine, beer, liquor, and brandy purchased by the landowner. They told of the many bands of musicians who would play and of the wandering jesters who had prepared brand new songs for the occasion and were already on a diet of whole bowls of fresh eggs to clear and tone up their voices, the eggs being furnished to the rich landowner by the hundreds of hens laying in his coops. The poor people swayed in their carriages, lashed their crippled little horses, and slobbered over their unkempt beards at the thought of the rich food being made ready by the millionaire in tens of giant pots for the traditional poor people's meal. Special klezmer bands will honour the poor. The bride herself, the only child, will dance a bride dance with the beggars' wives and seek their best wishes. The name of the patriarch on the groom's side, Yoshua Kutner, was not strange to them. Poor Jews had already encountered him and his greatness everywhere. In winter twilight, behind the hot ovens of the study houses, on Friday night by the doors of the *shuls* and in the stinking poor houses near the cemeteries, tales were told of Rabbi Kutner.

A few days before the wedding, the barns and stacks of hay and grain were already full of Jewish beggars. Their wagons stood among the court's carts and ploughshares. Grandfather Borukh laid everything open and instructed that they should be given as much bread and milk as they wanted. Hay should be given to the sick, hunched-over little horses tied up to the wagons. The little horses ate with gusto from the piles of fresh-smelling hay lying in abundance before them. They waved their tails happily and chased away the flies. The poor people felt at home, and the beggars' wives and daughters walked about freely in the orchard and picked apples and pears. Everything was allowed.

Chapter Nine

The Jewish beggar men and beggar women come to the meal for the poor. The poor and the cripples. In the orchard of Osmólsk. The poor eat the rich stew. Grandmother Khaye and the bride offer cake. Grandfather Borukh with a sack of copper coins. The poor people go dancing. The klezmer bands. Grandfather Borukh with an empty sack dances with the poor. The bride dances with the beggar women. Mazel tov.

Immediately after the male and female guests retired to rest, the maids and the Gentile girls of the 'court' began cleaning the tables and the orchard. The girls, knowing they were forbidden by Jewish law to touch the left-over bottles of wine, left them for the Jewish maids. The tables were soon cleared, and the maids shifted into setting places for the poor, that is, for the wedding meal for the travelling beggars.

Tablecloths that were put down now were dark and thick as sacks. The white tablecloths that the rabbis and their wives had eaten on had been removed. Deep earthenware bowls were put out, as well as earthenware jugs and cheap metal and wood cutlery. From the gates opening on the road to the court and from behind the fish-ponds and out from among the fruit trees, poor Jews came wearing tattered weekday garb smelling of sun and field. Whole packs of beggar women and girls began to gather in the court orchard. Some of the women had dirty children in their arms wrapped in rags. Grotesque and deformed

cripples crawled and hobbled among the women. Tall blind
beggars and scary blind women tried to steer correctly. They
warily tapped the ground and cried that people should not
abandon them. They also wanted to feast. The unkempt beards
of the poor folk shook on their grave, silent faces. The beggar
women had put on their shabby Sabbath dresses: long red and
flowered dresses, heads covered by white nightcaps or peasant
shawls. The girls also wore peasant shawls so that they would look
like married women instead of young girls. The whole company
of beggars moved towards the tables and silently took seats. The
cripples also took their seats. The blind tapped their sticks on the
shoulders of their confederates and plaintively cried that they
were hungry and should not be deserted. The poor people right
away picked up the wood and tin spoons and quietly drummed
them on the rude earthenware plates. Presently the Gentile girls
and Jewish cooks appeared on the steps of the court kitchen carrying big steaming pots. The keen smell of spiced and peppered
food filled the air, and the poor turned their gaze towards the
food. The men smothered their glee in their unkempt beards.
The young beggar women stood up on the benches, waved their
heads, and tried to signal to the maids to fill their bowls first.
They flourished their children wrapped in rags. The blind,
smelling the food, loudly knocked on the table with their sticks
and yelled that they were hungry. They groped in the air with
their hands and scraped the backs of their neighbours with their
fingers.

Servants emptied the pots into the earthenware bowls. Thick
steam emerged from the bowls. The poor began to drink the
broth loudly and greedily, and they chewed with their cheeks.
Some lifted the bones out of the broth and loudly cracked them
with their teeth, making animal sounds. Women poured spoon-
fuls of broth into the little mouths of the children and there and
then unbuttoned their bodices and nursed their infant children
while eating. The air filled with the knock of spoon and the
smack of lips and teeth. The blind anxiously sucked bones and
probed with their fingers in the bowls.

On the stairs appeared Grandfather Borukh, Grandmother

Khaye, the bride, and Aunt Royze with the bird on her cap and the Turkish shawl over her shoulders. They were carrying big baskets of cake. Grandfather also carried a sack full of copper coins.

Grandfather Borukh, Grandmother Khaye, and the bride walked around the eating poor people and showered big slices of cake and threw copper coins across the tables. The poor people caught the cake, stuffed it into their mouths, and snatched up the coins. The men, still eating, muttered blessings in their unkempt beards, and the older women loudly repeated old Jewish folk blessings and wished the dear bride all happiness, great *mazel*, long life, comeliness in the eyes of her husband, and God willing, the celebration of a circumcision in a year's time.

Afterwards, meat and *tsimmes* was brought out and tankards of beer. The poor drank the heavy, foamy drink and became merrier. Their faces shone because of the flush of the hot summer day, and the ample flecks of meat and *tsimmes* glistening on their cheeks. The moustaches of the men dripped with beer foam, and bits of cakes stuck to their beards along with crumbs of *tsimmes* and other delicacies. The poor people slowly crept out from behind the tables. Some unbuttoned their old torn long black coats and tipsily walked about on the grass. The children in rags at the breasts of their mothers fell into surfeited sleep. The women and the girls crept out from behind the tables and made a circle around the bride, continuing to tender good wishes. The blind alone stayed in their seats and poked their fingers around the emptied plates.

Dance! Dance! hoarsely cried the poor. And the women in the white nightcaps and flowered shawls on their heads also cried: Dance with the bride, dance with the dear bride!

The blind anxiously tapped the tables with their sticks.

Band musicians came from behind the trees. They were the most depressing and misfortunate musicians that the bands had sent to play for the poor. An old, lame, and half-blind musician with a bass fiddle. A tall, blond, tired, and emaciated musician with a flaking little yellow beard who listlessly carried a big tin trumpet. A ragged, barefoot boy lugged a drum, which looked to be bigger than he was. The poor folk saw them coming and ran to meet them. Many of the older women were dancing without even waiting for the music. The girls laughed. The women rocked their sleepy children on their breasts. The musicians apathetically arranged themselves behind a tree. First the half-blind bassist began to twang the bass tunelessly. The barefoot boy crazily and loudly drummed as though he was sounding an alarm. After a pause, as though suddenly coming awake, the blond trumpeter started to blow. His cheeks swelled up under the scraggly beard. The instruments, as though startled by each other, began to grow in intensity. A wild cacophony developed under the trees. The bass rumbled louder and louder and tried to out-rumble the drum. The air was shaken by the wild, disjointed chords, which did not blend together but nonetheless distantly recalled dance melodies. This drove the beggars wild. They had had a good meal and were suddenly in high spirits. They danced. The gloomy faces of the poor people broke into unwonted smiles. Unkempt beards quivered on their faces. The beggars spun about singly in the grass or joined hands and bounced into a circle dance. The women and the girls also spun around, leaping and clapping their hands to the sounds of the drum and trumpet. The blind smiled anxiously and palely, knocked their sticks over the tables, and yelled disquietingly: '*Mazel tov.*'

Soon Grandfather Borukh was surrounded by a gang of older beggars. Their torn long coats were carelessly unbuttoned. They tramped on the grass with their torn and dusty boots and caught Grandfather Borukh by the arms and pulled him into the circle. They put their hands on his new silk coat and held him by the shoulders. He still held the empty sack in which he had had the copper coins. A bit frightened, he let himself be drawn into the beggarly circle dance. The bride, too, was surrounded by a circle of beggar women in their nightcaps. Full of food, they smiled and clapped their hands and cried: '*Mazel tov*' and 'God willing, may there be a circumcision in a year's time.'

The bass was playing steadily louder, the drum drummed, the trumpet blew, and the blind tapped their long sticks on the tables.

Chapter Ten

The banquet for Grandfather's peasants. Peasants and peasant women in the colourful Łowicz costume. Peasant bands play mazurkas and wedding songs. The country uncles among the peasants. Uncle Mordekhai-Ber tells the peasants about the rabbis. Uncle Mordekhai-Ber would like to dance with a Gentile girl but fears Grandfather Borukh. The impoverished former landowner, land steward Gąsiorowski. The philosophy of a gentleman. The steward tells Uncle Leyzer Yosef stories over a glass of mead. The bride, Grandfather Borukh, and Grandmother Khaye among the peasants of Osmólsk. Country dances for the bride. Gąsiorowski dances with the bride. Uncle Mordekhai-Ber could not restrain himself anymore and snagged a Gentile girl to dance.

As soon as the paupers' meal came to an end, tables were set up near the barns to accommodate familiar peasants and farmhands. To celebrate the wedding, Grandfather Borukh wanted to make a banquet for them, too.

Country cakes and sweets were piled on the tables, and tall piles of apples and pears and big bottles of liquor. Casks of brandy also were placed nearby. The peasants, young boys and girls who worked at Grandfather's in the stables and barns and fields, poured in. The men wore the blue coats and coloured pants of the Łowicz area. The women and girls wore shawls and woollen dresses capturing the colours and moods of the Łowicz fields and landscape. They each wore many necklaces of colourful glass beads. The court smelt of cow dung and hay and the piles of apples and pears on the tables. A peasant band of fiddles, harmonicas, and flutes was off and away playing jovial mazurkas and Polish wedding songs. Male and female peasants performed Łowicz folk dances. Older peasants gossiped while standing about near the band and the dancers. The coach drivers told the others about the great rabbis whom they had driven and about the really young groom. 'Such a kid and so pale,' related the Gentile who had driven the carriage with R. Yoshua Kutner, as he wiped his long drooping moustache and added, 'But a great scholar. Our Miss will have an educated husband.' The old peasants nodded their heads. The uncles in their new long coats were at home among the peasants. Uncle Mordekhai-Ber in silk coat and skullcap explained the specific greatness of each rabbinical guest to the peasants and also the greatness of the Kalisher *rebetsn*, who lived in Warsaw and wrapped herself up every day in velvet and silk and ate nothing but butter cookies and coffee. With all six fingers he gave pregnant Aunt Genendl a mighty pinch on the behind under the attentive gaze of the peasants. His eyes under the velvet skullcap bulged like a wolf's as they wandered over the young Gentile girls dancing in bright Łowicz dresses and harkening to the lively music of the band. The feet of Uncle Mordekhai-Ber twitched, and he was in a mood to snag a girl and dance off with her as was his wont at the annual market in Osmolin, but he was spooked by the shining black silk coat he was wearing, and his nose still held the forbidding fragrance of the heavy coats and fur hats of the rabbis who had sat solemnly around the tables. And besides, he was scared to dance with a peasant woman at this moment in front of Grandfather Borukh as though it were just any market day! Today is the day before the wedding! Simkhe Gayge was nowhere to be seen. He was busy with the rabbis' wives. Uncle Leyzer Yosef, however, was outside the barn wearing a long silk coat and skullcap – Aunt Toybe was not with him at the moment – standing and talking with land steward Gąsiorowski.

Land steward Gąsiorowski was a ruined nobleman (I remember him from my childhood) who had dissipated his estates on horses and women. When Jewish moneylenders evicted him from his last estate, he decamped with the traditional costume of the gentry: the Polish sable hat, the stick with a big silver knob, the rifle, and the faithful dog Trezor, who never left him for a moment and followed his every step. This was all that remained of his former wealth. He bore his lot with the old fatalistic outlook of the Polish nobility. It bothered him not at all that in his old age he worked for a Jew. He would rather be the land steward of a Jew than the minion of a nouveau riche Polish bourgeois. With the pride of a member of his class, he hated peasants and the middle class but had nothing against the Jews, even though they had evicted him from his estate and had auctioned off his property. He said sincerely that such was the way of the world: an urban Christian becomes a shoemaker, a peasant receives thrashings, and a Jew stands about in a shop or lends money. So things have been from the six days of Creation and so they will be until the end of generations, and this scheme should not be altered in the least particular. Gąsiorowski was a devout Catholic, convinced that Providence knows best how to conduct the world and that the ideas of men are of no moment. Gąsiorowski had taken part in the Polish uprising of 1863, and his greatest pleasure was sitting with Uncle Leyzer Yosef over a glass of mead and telling about partisan battles with Cossacks in the deep and dark Polish woods. Gąsiorowski told tales of landowners and Jews hung by the Cossacks on trees. He also liked to tell tales from the good old times when a man could beat his peasants as much as he wished. At those sweet memories the old man's eyes moistened with feeling. He nervously twisted the tips of his long moustaches. Copious tears fell into his thick, dark mead. Uncle Leyzer Yosef, who had his own stories of the war in Pleven, never tired of hearing about Polish partisan battles in the woods, and his eyes too were moist with feeling as he plucked at his trimmed beard. The bonds of an intimate friendship grew slowly between the steward Gąsiorowski and Uncle Leyzer Yosef.

So the two stood now in the barnyard and gazed at the dancing peasants.

Gąsiorowski twisted the tips of his moustaches and told Uncle

Leyzer Yosef that in the old days when the peasants were thrashed, they were healthier and happier than now and the girls were firmer and prettier. Uncle Leyzer Yosef listened religiously.

When Grandfather Borukh, Grandmother Khaye, and the bride appeared in the barnyard, the band played a welcome. The peasants spread out; the teamsters and the herdsmen who tended Grandfather's cows and flocks of sheep cracked their long whips. Several of the village dogs barked from curiosity. The girls pelted the bride with blue field flowers and leaned down and put their arms around her legs. All cried out loudly, 'Long years,' while the band played more and more joyfully. Grandfather Borukh, Grandmother Khaye, and the uncles uncorked bottles of brandy and offered full tumblers. The peasants poured the liquor down their throats, wiped their moustaches, and bit into the sweet cakes and the wonderful-smelling apples and juicy pears. The steward Gąsiorowski slowly drank a glass of brandy and then went to the bride. His dog Trezor shadowed every step. Gąsiorowski's eyes were moist with feeling. He took the bride by the hand and tendered wishes in an old-fashioned Polish manner. Gąsiorowski had known the bride since her childhood because of his long years of acquaintance with Grandfather Borukh, and he addressed her by the familial *ty*.[1]

Soon the dances began again. The girls sang Polish wedding songs and danced around the bride. Here the steward could restrain himself in no longer. The old legs twitched as though rejuvenated by the beat of the music. He was reminded of the long-ago balls in his estates when he was famed as a first-class dancer. His eyes moistened and shone with an old nobleman's pride. He approached the bride. The dog Trezor followed his steps. Gąsiorowski bowed deeply before the bride like a cavalier and put his arm around her waist and elegantly led her into the dance.

At this point Uncle Mordekhai-Ber reached the limits of his endurance. His eyes shone like a wolf's. He hastily tore off the silk

---

1 Polish: 'you' (singular).

coat and tossed it to pregnant Aunt Genendl. Uncle Mordekhai-
Ber stood now only in trousers and braces and with a tall velvet
skullcap on his head. He rubbed his hands gleefully after the
peasant fashion and grabbed a girl from among the dancing
peasant couples and jolted with her into the circle.

The peasant band played more and more joyfully.

Chapter Eleven

Rabbi Gershon Henekh Radzyner. The Kotsker. Rabbi Mordekhai Yosef Izbitser the apostate. The Kotsker's misanthropic ways. Mice and frogs in the Kotsker's room. The Kotsker's evening meal. Hasidim feel estranged in Kotsk. The eloquent speaker Mordekhai Yosef. A kabbalistic revolutionary. Simchat Torah by the River Wieprz. The Hasidic revolution in Kotsk. The Kotsker's followers leave him. Rabbi Mordekhai Yosef. The Gostyniner recites psalms at a crossroad. The followers return. Rabbi Gershon Henekh the apostate grandchild. The genial dilettante. His extravagant ambitions. Rabbi Gershon Henekh envies the Rambam.[1] Rabbi Gershon Henekh finds the hillazon fish. His quarrels. Rabbi Gershon Henekh studies medical science with the local physician. R. Gershon Henekh and R. Yoshua Kutner. Gershon Henekh denounces all Polish Hasidic rabbis. How Rabbi Gershon Henekh wishes to greet the Messiah. Rabbi Gershon Henekh comes to my father's wedding. He wants to be with his enemies.

New relatives arrived on the morning of the wedding. There arrived the rebbe of Radzyń, Gershon Henekh, the one who had waged a bloody war with all the Polish Hasidim and rebbes over blue *tsitsis* and the hillazon fish, which he had discovered in the Mediterranean.

---

1 An acronym of Rabbi Moses ben Maimon, or Maimonides (1135–1204), one of the most outstanding Jewish philosophers and jurists. His commentary on the Mishna and his code Mishneh Torah constitute a brilliant systematization of Jewish law.

I wish to pause here for the purpose of writing about this rabbi.

Rabbi Gershon Henekh was a grandchild of the famous rabbi Mordekhai Yosef Izbitser.

Rabbi Mordekhai Yosef, who was numbered among the first and foremost Hasids of Kotsk, was also the man who did something of extraordinary rarity in the whole history of Hasidism. Hasidism was founded upon the authority of the *tsadik* and on blind faith in him and in his actions. On Simchat Torah in 1840, Rabbi Mordekhai Yosef led an open rebellion against his rabbi, the Kotsker. The revolt took place in Kotsk itself. While the Kotsker yet lived, Mordekhai Yosef pronounced himself rebbe and with virtually the whole congregation of Hasidim – who were in Kotsk at the time for a holiday – demonstratively left without a goodbye to the Kotsker. The leave-taking from one's rebbe is one of the chief acts of Hasidism. Mordekhai Yosef left Kotsk and began to 'practise' as rebbe in his hometown of Izbitsa.[2]

This wonderful and adventurous revolt is shrouded in a thousand veils. Among Polish Hasidim it was the theme of never-ending tales. Mordekhai Yosef was of a restless and temperamental nature. In addition, he had a penchant for kabbalistic mystical fantasy that fuelled still more his ambitions and disquiet. The chief cause of his insurgency, however, was as follows: the Kotsker had carried his misanthropic individualism to the level of isolation and bitterness and contempt for people. He locked himself in his room, rarely if ever admitted Hasidim, and embarked upon asceticism, which is exceptional among Hasidim. His words also rang like barbed aphorisms, and they flashed with brutal, deep wisdom that implicitly denigrated people. The wildest rumours circulated about the 'locked' years of the Kotsker. Hasidim were later to tell that the floor was never swept in the little room where the Kotsker spent his time. Large mice ran around freely. They became fat from the luxury. Old, grey, and ugly frogs jumped around the lonely Kotsker like trained dogs. It goes without saying that the Hasidim of Kotsk said that the mice and ugly frogs

---

2 Izbica, a small town fifty kilometres southeast of Lublin.

were really the souls of departed Hasidic sinners who had gone to the rabbi to bewail their needs in the next world and to ask him for improvement. The mice and frogs living with the Kotsker became so accustomed to their room-mate that when the Kotsker ate his one meal of the day at two in the morning (which incidentally was a chicken that had to be cooked for twenty-four hours until all its juices had melted away and only sort of withered flesh-grass was left on his plate), the well-fed mice and frogs encircled him, looked greedily straight into his eyes, croaked, and whistled, and he threw them breadcrumbs. These bold mice were also alleged to have eaten pieces of the Kotsker's long coat and even to have dared to bite him in the face. No one was allowed to chase away these ugly and weird creatures. The Kotsker fell into a rage whenever someone interfered with his room-mates, and the assailant was cursed with deadly imprecations. The Kotsker considered these undesirables the only beings with which a recluse could interact. However much or little these legends were factually true, they – like legends in general – contained a core of truth: they captured the misanthropic attitude of the Kotsker towards his followers and his general world view. In addition to all this was a truly remarkable fact: the Kotsker became a widower in the midst of his ascetic-misanthropic period and married a young virgin, a great beauty and the daughter of a rich man from Warsaw, Reb Moshe Chalfan.[3] Another son-in-law of Moshe Chalfan was the future Gerer rebbe.[4] Exactly a year after the wedding, the ascetic Kotsker celebrated the first circumcision.

For one part of his followers the extraordinary contradictions in the Kotsker's behaviour only added to his authority and magnetism. Hasiduth emphasized the idea of trust in authority. The unconditional believers transformed all the shadowy sides of the Kotsker into major, secret-filled lights. In the rabbi's presence they were in seventh heaven, for all that this 'heaven' was sar-

---

3 'Chalfan' in Hebrew is a money-changer.
4 The Gerer Hasidim originated among former Kotsker Hasidim.

donic and sealed-off under lock and key. They thought the
Kotsker's ways had hidden holiness. His path was a tangle of different things. It belonged to a different dimension from simplis-
tic human thinking and contained great symbolic meaning. But
a faction of the Hasidim could not understand the blatant contradictions. They were sickened that the Kotsker shrank from
every interaction with them. He cursed and swore at them and
showed at every turn his contempt for humanity. Many minds
among the Kotsk Hasidim became uneasy, minds which were
accustomed to togetherness and a deep spiritual linkage.
Nagging grains of doubt and dissatisfaction began to grow about
the Kotsker. They began to feel like a deserted flock of sheep.
The essence of Hasidism is the sense of community, a sense of
community that in its most extreme form expresses itself through
the mystical authority of the *tsadik*.

As I've said already, the Izbitser rebbe was of a very restless and
rebellious nature. He seethed with an apostate's obsessive imagination, which no sooner had reservations about a spiritual path
than it went to work and came up with a mental picture of the
problematic path that was far off the mark. Then, too, Reb
Mordekhai Yosef was an excellent conversationalist, loving to talk
and preach Hasidism. The Hasidim were brothers to him, and he
regularly joined them in mystical communion. This alienated
him even more from the Kotsker's standoffishness. If one of the
Hasidic students tried to explain the Kotsker's eccentric habits by
saying that he had been elevated to the rank of an angel and
behaved like one, Mordekhai Yosef answered sarcastically that
there were enough angels in heaven and here on earth what was
needed was a rabbi to study with his Hasidim – and what sort of a
rebbe is the Kotsker who runs away from people and sits among
frogs and mice? An antisocial rebbe who creeps around in dust
and spiderwebs and curses with deadly maledictions and at the
same time – how remarkable! – shows great tenderness to his
young and lovely wife. Who can travel alongside the Kotsker
through the desert of these contradictions! To study and converse with Hasidim and be forever united in a spiritual community – this was the core of Hasidism and also the core of

Mordekhai Yosef's fantasy-filled temperament. He lived in a community and treated it like a real revolutionary.

Mordekhai Yosef's temperament was further exacerbated by the Kabbalistic images that filled his thoughts. Every gesture he saw around himself, every verse he learned from Scripture, every Kabbalistic reckoning of the numerical value of words suggested ultimately what was already in the nether regions of his subconsciousness, namely, apostasy. He believed himself to be called from heaven to perform the great mission of becoming the leader of the forsaken Hasidim, who would leave the Kotsker to his mice and his misanthropy. Mordekhai Yosef's book *Waters of Siloam,* which his grandson Reb Gershon Henekh published, is full of mystical and erotic symbolism. So too in this book is to be discerned a great revolutionary and independent thinker who prefers radical and rebellious contradictions. For example, Korah figures in the Bible as the incorrigible rebel against Moses. In the Talmud and in all of Jewish religious literature he is considered the epitome of sinfulness. In his book *Waters of Siloam,* Mordekhai Yosef defends Korah against the charge. He tries to show that Korah was a great man and great mystic and that his revolt against Moses was inspired by mystic visions and had deep Kabbalistic meanings; that the story of Korah was not so simple and that his battle with Moses had a background of great mysteries. Rabbi Mordekhai Yosef had much in him of the Jewish Neoplatonists of antiquity. They also turned every word of the Tanakh[5] into a thousand occult allusions, and they also read reality as a magic book of symbols. It is not necessary to be a great psychoanalyst to discern in the mystical-revolutionary tack and in the esoteric and symbolic apologetics for Korah both the entire psychic mechanism of Mordekhai Yosef's restless and domineering character and a defence of his own rebellion. He suffered from a deep feeling of guilt, as well as a gnawing ambition for power.

---

5 An acronym used in the Jewish tradition for the Hebrew Bible: Torah, Neviim, and Ketuvim (Pentateuch, Prophets, and Writings).

We have little information about that time as to how and in what manner the remarkable Izbitser revolution was prepared. Dissatisfaction and the bizarre alienness of the Kotsker himself must have created a revolutionary atmosphere. No doubt, R. Mordekhai Yosef for his part did all he could to sharpen the dissatisfaction. He was a master of conversation, probably very lively and imaginative conversation, which had a great impact on the Hasidim of Kotsk, who had arrived there fraught with yearnings and longings.

From the Kotsker's dusty and spiderweb-covered room there came a steady stream of outlandish rumours – rumours that fanned the flames still more and overcast the anxious spirits. People said that the Kotsker threw his *tefillin*[6] on the ground and that he lit a candle on the very Sabbath and still other equally appalling stories. They surely did not correspond to the reality since, despite all his radical individualism, the Kotsker was strictly orthodox in regard to the Shulkhan Arukh.[7] He was a great adherent of the Torah and all its rules and laws, and he deeply respected Talmudic scholars and prodigies. It must be remembered that at the time the bizarre reverberations from the Sabbatai Zvi[8] and above all the Jacob Frank[9] incidents still lay heavily in the air of Polish Jewry, and such rumours about one whose conduct began to be very contradictory, very peculiar, and mysterious fell on very receptive soil. Everything could have been easily explained by the lurid imagination of the Hasidim. Their minds were inclined to be obsessed with real possibilities that had already happened and could occur again. The Hasidim themselves then lived on the narrow margin between tradition and the

---

6 Small, black leather, cube-shaped boxes containing Torah texts and worn during the daily morning service.
7 Rabbi Joseph Caro's classic codification of Jewish law, which has been the Orthodox standard since the sixteenth century.
8 A Turkish Jew (1626–76) who declared himself the Messiah and developed a mass movement, which was reduced to a small sect after his apostasy and death.
9 A Polish Jewish messianic pretender (1726–91) who claimed that he was the reincarnation of Sabbatai Zvi. In 1758–9 he presided over his followers' mass apostasy in converting formally to Catholicism.

lack of tradition; for all of their piety, they had loosened the
fetters of the Law. They were conservative revolutionaries and
dreamers looking for novelty in their own inner lives. Conservative revolution is a stick with two ends. A stick with two ends can
be an effective weapon, but it menaces him who carries it and
uses it during his life's journey.

After the meal on Simchat Torah, Mordekhai Yosef and all of
the community who were present at the time in Kotsk went down
to the River Wieprz. It was his habit to walk about the area with
groups of Hasidim and engage them in his famous discussions.
The air of tension in Kotsk had by then come to a head.
Mordekhai Yosef must have demanded that the Hasidim take a
momentous step and break with the Kotsker, and it seems that his
imaginative eloquence and nervous energy were at their shining
peak, for he prevailed. His will was done. The die was cast and all
the bridges were burned. When the Hasidim went back to their
lodgings towards evening, it was known that it would happen
tomorrow. The Kotsker was being abandoned in misanthropic
isolation; he was left in spiderwebs with the mice and the frogs
and with his curses, bitter as those of Timon of Athens.[10] The
living people were leaving him. A new light of learning was being
lit in Izbitsa.

And thus it happened: on the morning of the day after the
holiday, Rabbi Mordekhai Yosef set out for Izbitsa with the whole
crowd. As I have already recounted, nobody even bid farewell to
the Kotsker. The act of not taking leave from the rebbe expressed
the high point of the revolt.

Kotsk stood empty. As Hasidim tell it, the Kotsker was shocked
by Mordekhai Yosef's deed. In his isolation he must have been
unaware of what was brewing around him. He is said to have
cursed Mordekhai Yosef with desolate curses. In light of which
Mordekhai Yosef said, upon seeing a beam fall from the ceiling of
a roadside inn where he stayed with the Hasidim for the night,
'The Kotsker shoots beams but I'm not afraid.'

---

10 A Greek sceptic philosopher (320–230 BC).

The rumour of the rebellion in Kotsk spread to all the Kotsker prayer houses in Poland. Nearly all of the Kotsker Hasidim supported going over to the apostate of Izbitsa. Even the holy rabbi of Gostynin. The rabbi of Gostynin, a Kotsker Hasid, went there a few days after the events in Kotsk. On the way he heard what had happened. The holy rabbi of Gostynin was later to say that, while driving a cart, he came to a crossroad. The sandy Polish roads split: one fork led to Kotsk and the other to Izbitsa. He climbed down from his cart and recited psalms, hoping that the Master of the Universe would enlighten him and show him the right path to follow. It so happened that the choice fell on Kotsk, and so the rabbi of Gostynin continued on the road there. When he arrived, everything was vacant, the prayer house empty, the Kotsker angry, isolated, and cursing continuously. Only Rabbi Itskhok Meir, the Hidushei ha-Rim, and a few others of the faithful stood by the abandoned rebbe.

What is remarkable is this: the great majority of the defectors returned one by one to Kotsk. Once the great deed was achieved, the Izbitser exerted himself but fell exhausted and began to flicker out. The Hasidim who had left with him had begun to be disappointed. It might also have been that at the end of the day conservative and traditional feelings won out in their hearts. The Kotsker's authority revived in their bosoms and the fugitives broke down under it. Their apostasy didn't stand the test of time. The overwhelming majority of the so-called apostates returned to Kotsk and became even fiercer Kotsker Hasidim than they were before. With his contradictions and sharp-witted misanthropy, the eccentric Kotsker began all of a sudden to seem rather charming. The only lasting effect of the whole revolution was that Poland gained a small rabbinical dynasty, that of Izbitsa. Mordekhai Yosef as rebbe played a part quite different from the part he had played in opposition. There exist spirits who can only be creative as antitheses. Mordekhai Yosef shone impressively only as the antithetical foil to the remarkable personality of the Kotsker. For the next twenty years, the years of his true greatness, the Kotsker remained locked up in his unswept little chamber and fed the mice and the frogs at two o'clock in the morning with the crumbs of his meagre meal and cursed his most devoted adherents with deadly curses. Out of these misanthropic years flowed his greatest impact on the character of the Kotsk Hasidim. The memory and influence of the Kotsker were much stronger in Polish Hasidism than the impact of the eloquent and witty Izbitser.

After R. Mordekhai Yosef died, his son Yankele ascended to the rabbinical chair in Izbitsa. There was little in him of his revolutionary father. His was a quiet, lyrical, and poetic nature. His book *Bet-Yaakov* (*The House of Jacob*) is one of the most beautiful mood books of Hasidic literature.

R. Gershon Henekh had much of his grandfather Mordekhai Yosef in him.

R. Gershon certainly lacked the deep mystical fire of his grandfather. He did not have the visionary kabbalistic outlook on all and everything. On the contrary, R. Gershon was a thoroughgoing rationalist with little fantasy and vision. And yet he had his grandfather's rebelliousness and apostasy and will to fight and oppose, but in his particular case these characteristics did not express themselves in flights of fantasy. Neither did he have the opportunity to make a splash as a fomenter of rebellion that his grandfather had. After all Mordekhai Yosef had taken on such a luminary as the Kotsker because the Kotsker invited mockery and a contest for his chair. R. Gershon had no such golden opportunity for confrontation. The dynasty of Izbitsa was second-rate and played but a scant part in the historical development of Hasidism in Poland, while the influence of the Kotsker was enormous. The dynasties directly descending from Kotsk, such as Ger, for instance, were in the foreground of Hasidic life. R. Gershon Henekh was a latter-day revolutionary without an outlet through which to discharge his mutinousness. Therefore – psychological laws! – his apostate qualities changed into wild ambitions. Even rather naive and dilettantish ambitions. The sickly bitterness of an unrealized greatness spoke from him in deed, in word, and in writing. Gershon Henekh was certainly unusually bright. Perhaps even a genius. His soured ambitions overruled everything else. Everything he did – and did

largely amateurishly – was done to win attention, to outdo everyone, and above all – and here he really got carried away – to
surpass his grandfather. He wanted each of his deeds to be loud,
original, and innovative and – most importantly – insulting, to
demonstrate his superiority over the whole world of rabbis and
rebbes in Poland and to dumbfound everyone. Although R.
Gershon Henekh provoked the sharpest opposition against
himself, it did not frighten him but only served to strengthen his
driving urges and his ambitious belief in himself. The hatred
towards him was oil poured on the flames of his ambition.
Intransigent conflict harked back to the primal scene of R.
Mordekhai Yosef's war with the Kotsker, and that was the ideal
that Gershon Henekh always worked towards. He was forever
saddling himself with surprising and spectacular tasks. For
instance: the Mishnah has six orders. The Talmudic commentaries on the Mishnah – which were assembled over a period of
two to three centuries – treat four of the orders only. There are
no traces of commentary on the Order of Purification (Taharot)
in the Mishnah, and so R. Gershon Henekh undertook to do it
himself, a gigantic task requiring the work of generations. He
did in fact finish one 'tractate' and published it. Rabbinical cri-
tique praised the daring of his undertaking but on the whole
severely criticized the work, pointing out colossal errors and
calling it the befuddled work of a dilettante. I do not feel quali-
fied to take a stand on the matter, but somehow I feel that at play
in the negative reception of his work must have been R. Gershon
Henekh's poor relationships with everyone, his quarrels with
everyone, and the fact that he besmirched the names of the
greatest scholars of his day, both in speech and in writing. I am
a critic myself and know how large a role subjective attitude can
play in critical evaluation.

R. Gershon Henekh went on to create even more havoc in the
rabbinical and Hasidic world. This is what happened. In the
Talmud there is a legend that the hillazon fish, whose blood is
used to dye blue one of the prescribed eight tassels (*tsitsit*), sur-
faces from the depths of the sea once every seventy years.
Tremendous knowledge is required to ensnare it since it involves

calculating when the fish will appear. This esoteric knowledge was one of the secrets of the high priests of the Temple that was lost in the destruction of Jerusalem. We do not know when the hillazon fish shows itself or how to catch it. The post-destruction generations have had to do without the blood of this fish just as they have had to do without Temple sacrifices. But what's lost is lost. These are bitter times, and for the hillazon fish one will have to wait until the coming of the Messiah. So say the Talmudic legends, more or less, but for such an obstinate and contrary creature as R. Gershon Henekh this was hardly an answer. He was not going to have sand thrown in his eyes and wait – a detail – for the Messiah to arrive. On the contrary, the legends awoke an itch in him to find the fish himself and to show up everybody. Triumph, of course, was not long in coming. The exciting news reached R. Gershon Henekh in Radzyń, although it was well known to anyone with even a smattering of zoology that ink fish are in the Mediterranean Sea or the Gulf of Naples, more accurately. Today this ink fish is to be found in every good-sized aquarium. R. Gershon Henekh did not brood long. He made a special trip to Naples to see the ink fish, but he did not check the fish's passport about whether it spends seventy years at a stretch in the dark depths of the sea or ever had professional dealings with the priests of the Temple. Right there and then he ruled that this was the sought-after hillazon fish, so no longer any need to wait for the Messiah. From now on Jews would have to go back to wearing blue *tsitstit* as in the times of the Temple. Enough pampering.

This created real turmoil in the rabbinical world. Once again the hated R. Gershon astounded people, and once again he did so by flouting all accepted legends. How is it possible? How could this be the creature that rises from the depths only once in seventy years according to a timetable that only the priests knew, just as they alone knew how to ensnare the elusive fellow? Look what muddles ensued from Gershon Henekh's ambitions! The fish he brought back from Italy and showed that it carries blue dye in its pouch was all in all an empty mystification, a bastard fish. The ink compromises the kosher validity of the other *tsitsit*.

The hatred of R. Gershon Henekh felt by all the giants of the Torah, whom he had constantly attacked personally and insulted orally and also in print in the tractate on the Seder Taharot that he had compiled, aggravated the resistance to the hillazon fish and made it personal and nasty.

It hardly needs to be said that R. Gershon Henekh was not a man to run from polemics. He became more cheerful, more stubborn, and more abusive. R. Gershon Henekh took the public stage, both orally and in writing, to defend his breakthrough and hit back at his critics. He girded his loins with scholarly casuistry and pointed to Talmudic proofs of his thesis as well as proofs from the later gaonim and authorities. A wild feud broke out between Gershon Henekh and his Hasidim on one side and the whole Hasidic and rabbinical world on the other. All the Radzyner Hasidim donned the blue *tsitsit* at the behest of R. Gershon Henekh. They were attacked and beaten by other Hasidim, mainly the Hasidim of Ger. As I will later relate, the Gerer Hasidim bore a particularly intense hatred towards R. Gershon Henekh. All hell broke loose in those Polish shtetls where any of his Hasidim lived. Their little prayer rooms were attacked; their means of livelihood taken away; they were denounced to the local authorities; wives divorced their husbands; fathers banished their sons-in-law. It was riotous. Writing and polemics against Gershon Henekh sprang up like mushrooms after rain. They produced no results: R. Gershon Henekh stubbornly clung to his belief that his hillazon fish is the hillazon fish and thumbed his nose at everyone. The Radzyners still wear the blue *tsitsit* to this day and look exotic and peculiar in the eyes of other Hasidim.[11]

Right after the hillazon fish controversy, R. Gershon Henekh commenced hostilities, as I have already told, against *etrogim* from the Land of Israel and against non-Jewish maids. He also conducted these wars with the greatest acrimony and personal attacks on everyone and everybody. He applied ugly nicknames to

---

11 The blue-dyed fringe is also fashionable in some modern Orthodox, religious Zionist Jewish circles.

the greatest authorities among Polish Hasidic rebbes. Most of his attacks were directed at the Gerer rebbe. The Gerer dynasty descended lineally from that of Kotsk. Probably, the psychological motive that drove R. Gershon Henekh to take up the gauntlet and pursue a war against Kotsk was that it allowed him to be compared with his grandfather. I will tell more about his feud with Ger later on.

His insatiable ambitions were released not only in the fields of the Torah and Hasidism. As we know, R. Gershon Henekh had taken R. Mordekhai Yosef as a personal model, but then his ambitions reached ever higher and further. No less than Maimonides was the secret measure of his ambition. R. Gershon Henekh had organized his commentary on the Order of Purity to have the earmarks of what Maimonides had accomplished in his Mishneh Torah. Who knows what Gershon Henekh thought about himself or what exaggerated idea of his own abilities led him to pit himself against Maimonides. But it was not enough, for Maimonides was still more than a commentator; he was the court physician of the caliph in Cairo. This was fodder for the jealousy that stabbed the insatiable dilettante.

R. Gershon Henekh got hold of several old medical booklets in Hebrew and also invited the doctor of the little town of Radzyń to pay a call. This rabbinical Don Quixote, who was undoubtedly someone to be reckoned with as a rabbi and rebbe, wanted to electrify the world all over again, and this time not only the Torah study hall crowd but the world at large. He would study medical science without the help of universities or formal courses. Here too he would exceed everybody. Here too he would have monumental fame and gain himself glory and foes.

R. Gershon Henekh had provincial, fanciful, and amateurish conceptions of modern science, so success here did not take long. His Hebrew medical books and the provincial doctor were not themselves oversupplied with knowledge, so they did not make it hard for the talented amateur to become a medical expert. In no time at all he began convincing his Hasidim that in a brief time he had become one of Poland's best-informed doctors and began writing prescriptions left and right.

This latest 'achievement' did not cause the same sensation in the Jewish world as the earlier quixotic feats, and Gentile ears did not even hear a rumour of the new medical star in the Radzyner study hall. Perhaps the rebbes believed him.

The only rabbinical authority in Poland whom R. Gershon Henekh placed higher than himself and who was not a bitter pill for him to swallow was Rabbi Yoshua Kutner. He accepted everything from the Kutner, both the pleasant and the unpleasant. He often went to visit R. Yoshua in Kutno. He approached him with respect and reverence.

My father saw him in Kutno at R. Yoshua's. Although my father was a still a young fellow, he found high favour with R. Gershon Henekh, who talked to him like a grown-up and even confided his inner thoughts to him. R. Yoshua was drawn to the Radzyner rabbi with a certain genial sympathy one might feel for a talented amateur. He didn't think much of Gershon Henekh's books and considered the hillazon commotion a childish stunt. My father told me that R. Gershon Henekh travelled by himself and did without an attendant, which in those days was quite daring for a Hasidic rabbi. He did so only to show up his rabbinical colleagues. When my father asked him (when in Kutno, R. Gershon Henekh slept in the same room as my father, which provided a setting for relaxed and intimate conversations) why he travelled without an attendant against all accepted customs and against the 'court etiquette' of Hasidic rebbes, R. Gershon Henekh answered sarcastically that he did not need a 'bear trainer.' That was not enough; he then enumerated a whole roll of living savants of the Polish Hasidim who could not move without a 'bear trainer.' And why was this? Because they were good-for-nothings, cripples, idlers, and anything else bad that you can think of. His most biting words and worst scorn fell naturally on the head of the Gerer rebbe, his greatest rival and the legal heir of Kotsk. R. Gershon Henekh insultingly called him 'Deaf Leybush' because the Gerer rabbi was a little deaf in one ear.

Also, travelling to Ciechocinek,[12] R. Gershon Henekh would

---

12 A spa close to the city of Toruń.

stop in at R. Yoshua Kutner's, which was on the way. R. Gershon
Henekh did not wear the famous long silk jacket of Hasidic Jews
but a simple long, grey non-religious duster coat. This also
evoked bitter commentary from his enemies. Polish rabbis and
Hasidim were extremely strict about maintaining traditional
clothing and they classified the least deviation as 'Gentile ways.'
My father told me the following remarkable fact: R. Gershon
Henekh was once unpacking his suitcase and in it lay a revolver.
My father, a Hasidic young fellow, became frightened and asked
R. Gershon Henekh why he needed such an implement of
destruction. 'To greet the Messiah,' sarcastically answered R.
Gershon Henekh. 'One must greet the Messiah like a real man.
Who is going to greet him? Those good-for-nothings, cripples,
and idlers?' And he went through the list of living rabbinical
authorities. R. Gershon Henekh added that since his blood
enemies, the Gerer Hasidim, considered him fair game, he had
to be able to protect himself. R. Gershon Henekh asked my
father not to tell R. Yoshua Kutner about the revolver 'because
the old fellow will get scared.' I think that all these fantasies must
have derived from a persecution mania linked to his unsatisfied
ambitions. The morbid ambitions of megalomania and a sense of
persecution often go hand in hand.

When R. Gershon Henekh died, Gerer Hasidim in many towns
drank a toast to his death, whooped it up, and danced in the
prayer halls. The amateur genius moved in such an atmosphere
of hatred. But I will not go further into the matter.

Gershon Henekh came to my father's wedding for two reasons.
One was because of his friendship with R. Yoshua Kutner and the
second, perhaps, to have the great pleasure of being with his
enemies, the other rabbis and rebbes at the wedding. He liked to
feel on himself the looks of hatred of his bitter foes. It gave him
pleasure.

Chapter Twelve

The day of the wedding ceremony. The bride fasts. Grandmother Khaye among the rabbis and the rebbes. Grandmother Khaye conjures away the evil eye and counts the pennies for charities. Plea for mercy. Simkhe Gayge runs to the tsadikim in the orchard and asks for remedies. Aunt Royze works wonders. Torah and casuistic debate in the Osmólsk orchard. Hirshl with the Gemara and with water bottles walks around among the fruit trees. Simkhe Gayge is punished by Hirshl. Wedding food is being cooked in the kitchen. Strumming musical instruments under the fruit trees. Noah Nashelsker rehearses.

The summery Tamuz day of the marriage ceremony turned out hot and bright. The skies shone in their dark-bluishness. The sun was full of colour like a golden ship. Warm smells of harvest wafted from the fields from the ripened corn, from wheat just ripening, from oats and barley. Birds twittered in the warm air. In-laws continued to stream in.

The groom and the bride had to fast through a long and hot summer day. Among the Hasidic rebbes, amid the rustle of the black silken rabbinical house coats and long gabardines, Grandmother Khaye felt like a fish in water. All her superstitions surfaced. She felt that all the holy heavens to which she prayed at New Year from her old tear-stained prayer book, for whom she lit great wax candles on Yom Kippur and recited special women's prayers for the God-fearing heavens of the Days of Awe, had opened over her house. The holy angels out of the Jewish women's prayer book were circulating here invisible among so many rabbis and rebbes. Just imagine! She had lived to experience the great honour of seeing with her own eyes so many holy men. She felt unworthy of it and feared the evil eye for herself, for her husband, and for the sole dear daughter left out of so many children. The only child is now having her wedding day and fasting. Grandmother Khaye had all her life dreaded the evil eye, and for the scantiest of reasons – say, when someone yawned in her presence – she immediately spat nine times and said various incantations in Ivri-Taytsh,[1] incomprehensible even to herself. She then licked her daughter's eyes seven times and spat on her own fingers. Besides, Grandmother Khaye had had a few thousand pennies already spoken for. These were wrapt in several old flowery Łowicz kerchiefs and in special sheet-metal pots. Each Rosh Hashanah eve, she counted the pennies while whispering incantations that she knew by heart. Goes without saying that on the day of the marriage ceremony of the so much-feared-for daughter she carefully counted the pennies once again, rewrapped them in the Łowicz kerchiefs, and said the appropriate incantations with special earnestness. And while doing so, Grandmother Khaye wept buckets of tears. Her pale face was wet from tears the whole day through, and her eyes were red from incessant quiet weeping. True, she knew that on this day she was protected by the presence of the many pious men who were under her roof, but who can be protected against an evil eye? And one must be on guard at all times and beg for mercy and do what one can. The bride is pale from fasting and can be expected to swoon at any moment. And the bride also weeps all day as today is the day of her marriage ceremony and the day of marriage is equal to Yom Kippur and the book of her life is especially open in heaven and angels are holding goose-feather quills in hand ready to write. No joking matter this, the day of the marriage canopy. All day long Grandmother Khaye continued to

---

1 Literally 'Hebrew-Translation,' the archaic Yiddish dialect used in old religious texts.

send messengers to different *tsadikim* to remember the bride
kindly on the day of the ceremony and also not to be sparing with
remedies. However many remedies Simkhe Gayge brought back,
she did not feel them to be adequate. Simkhe Gayge, who already
considered himself to be a part of the *tsadikim,* gladly ran errands
to them with fresh demands again and again and begged for
mercy in his coarse peasant voice. He had to get used to *tsadikim*
and sounded a bit uncouth, but he accepted the fine, delicate
voices from the saintly throats of the *tsadikim.* Although he understood but little of the Hebrew words spoken to him, nevertheless
he felt confident and at home among them and his reddish eyes
sparkled with pleasure. Simkhe was leaving the rabbis' wives and
Grandmother Khaye more often and longer to inhale with his
flared peasant nostrils the sharp pepper-like smell of the rabbinic
fur hats and of the heavy silk house coats.

Nor was Aunt Royze silent, with the Turkish shawl on her back
and the cap on her head. She brought with her from home some
burnt-out pieces of waxen Yom Kippur candles which she had
been collecting for years. These she lit in the bride's room. The
sweet smell of wax wafted in the room, and Grandmother Khaye
and Aunt Royze grimaced, said special women's prayers over the
dripping Yom Kippur candles, gestured with their hands as
though lighting the candles for the Sabbath, and continually
exorcised the bride against the evil eye.

R. Yoshua Kutner and the great and well-known rabbis who had
come to the wedding were all, on account of the hot day, strolling
about in the orchard among the apple, pear, and plum trees. The
air reverberated with a sharp Talmudic dispute, barely audible.
Questions were asked and answers given. The leaves rustled over
the apples and the pears. Mild breezes blew from the grain fields.
Birds sang in the air. And the most select quotations from the
Talmud and rabbinic legal works flew around the scholars like
wild sharp birds in contrast to the ripe, fragrant summer day and
the smells that drifted down from the fruit trees, in contrast to
the smells of the ripe apples and of the ripe pears. R. Yoshua
Kutner conquered everyone with his brilliance, and the great
rabbis wearing colourful silk house coats and large skullcaps on

their heads finally stopped, exhausted. The strongest had been the 'Living Soul,' for his strength in casuistic dispute was also very great. He alone remained with R. Yoshua on the battlefield, but he too finally gave in. Hirshl brought out big Talmuds in which to look and to check. In the pockets of his seven long coats he carried around bottles of water, and he poured water over the hands of one rabbi after another, spilling some over their silken coats. Hirshl moved among the warring great scholars of the Torah with audacious familiarity, like one of them. Although he understood not a word, the rapid and strange sounds did not rest in his overgrown ears as alien sounds, for he had become accustomed to them. Wherever he went, he emitted the foul smell of the Kutno butcher shops, but he paid no mind.

Here, then, even as the sharp arrows of casuistic dispute flew about, the message was delivered by Simkhe Gayge from Grandmother Khaye to remember the fasting bride. R. Yoshua Kutner was enmeshed together with the other rabbis in the exotic and dry sounds of Torah novellas, and they had all become entangled in an incomprehensible language. It frightened the healthy and peasant-like Simkhe Gayge. The sturdily built village Jew stood there helpless like a child and babbled something to a rabbi in a red silken house coat. The rabbi was listening to R. Yoshua and impatiently finished off Simkhe with a quick scholarly quote. Simkhe coughed, blinked his eyes, and swallowed spittle. The incomprehensible remarks from the rabbi stuck in his throat like a dry chip not to be swallowed. Hirshl, who was waddling about among the scholars with two uncorked water bottles and with a big thick Talmud volume under his arm, angrily chased Simkhe away, looking him over sternly with his one eye. Simkhe Gayge resignedly gestured with his hand and returned to the rabbis' wives. From the open windows of the court kitchen came the sharp smell of onions and peppered fish. The stuffed pike, the peppered carp, the fat crucian carp and tench were being cooked in big copper kettles. Whole flocks of geese were baking in brownish fat, and the well-fed and fattened hens and turkeys were cooking in pots. Turmoil reigned in the kitchen, where sharp damp heat mixed with sweet and piquant smells of the wedding dishes. Mountains of oak logs flickered in the oven like hellish fire from Gehenna. To the great heat of the summer day was added the heat of the burning oven. Copper kettles and pots were boiling on the gleaming stovetops. Jewish cooks from Kutno and Łowicz stood about with wooden spoons, mixing, removing the scum from the chicken broth, and constantly tasting the dishes with the tips of their tongues. Along the long table stood the Gentile girls, heads covered with colourful Łowicz kerchiefs, as they peeled carrots and chopped parsley and onions. Their cheeks burned and their eyes glistened from the chopped onions. Great heat emanated from the white tiled oven, as large heaps of white rolls, sugar and honey cakes, almond tortes, and other sweet and juicy confections were all baked there. Servers in black coats and wearing black skullcaps moved among the cooks and the Gentile girls. They yelled in Yiddish and in Polish. The peasant girls peeled carrots and chopped onions and laughed at the younger waiters. In the rooms, long wedding-feast tables were being set out.

From beyond the orchard trees were heard snatches of the strumming of instruments. Snatches of jesters' typical motifs were audible, including the golden lion's roar of Noah Nashelsker. Rehearsals were taking place. The jesters attempted to adapt their poems and sayings into the music of the bands.

Chapter Thirteen

The expensive wedding dress from Warsaw. Simkhe Gayge brings the wedding dress. Grandmother Leah and the Kalisz rabbi's wife show what they are capable of doing. Dressing of the bride. The bands play a quadrille. Girls dance before the bride.

Later in the afternoon commenced the dressing of the bride in her wedding gown and veils. In a large room in the 'court,' the local women gathered along with the rabbis' wives and female wedding guests. Grandmother Khaye's eyes were tear-stained. Aunt Ratse in her Turkish shawl carried a frying pan containing a variety of smoking elixirs, incense, and olive oils. She continually repeated incantations against the evil eye and spat in all directions. Simkhe Gayge brought in the long white silken wedding gown, which had been custom-made in Warsaw by the foremost seamstress in accordance with the latest fashion. Simkhe Gayge carried the dress gingerly with both hands and with his whole body, barely daring to put his foot down so as not to let, Heaven forbid, the dress fall and be damaged. When Grandmother Leah and the Kalisz *rebetsn* took the wedding dress off his hands, he heaved a huge sigh, loudly blew his nose, and dried big drops of sweat with his sleeve.

Grandmother Leah and the Kalisz rabbi's wife spread the white silk wedding gown across several chairs, which were covered with a white tablecloth. Only someone from Warsaw, one who has previously seen great sumptuous weddings of the wealthy of Warsaw and the wedding gowns of the rich Warsaw brides, could find a way in the whole delicate, airy, and complicated structure of the gown. The gown grunted angrily at the slightest touch and the slightest movement, as though refusing to be touched by just anybody, and oozed big-city pride and proud heritage. The fabrics, pleats, ribbons, and trains gleamed with dead pale whiteness like dried lily petals, enveloped in coils of lace and tulle.

Grandmother Leah and the rabbi of Kalisz's wife consulted with one another on how to find a way in the chaotic maze of cloth, trains, and little hooks. Slowly they unbuttoned the dress. Other women had in the meantime divested the bride of her everyday clothes. The bride, pale from fasting, weak, and frightened, willingly placed herself in their hands. Grandmother Khaye wept, stroked the bride's village braids, and gave her bottles of smelling salts as on Yom Kippur. Aunt Royze in the meantime did what she could, burning incense and exorcising the evil eye. When the bride was half undressed and Grandmother Leah and the rabbi of Kalisz's wife were ready with the wedding gown, the bride was dressed in white lacy petticoats, white silken hose, and white silk shoes brought from Warsaw. Grandmother Leah and the rabbi of Kalisz's wife set to putting the gown on the bride.

The gown rustled proudly at every movement and like a white mist swathed the girlish body of the young village bride. The ribbons and trains rustled and streamed around her hands, her throat, and around her waist like light fantastic leaves and skeins dancing in the wind. The pale bride was lost in the elegant profusion of fabrics. The face, pale from fasting, was of the same hue as the fabric. The bride in the wedding gown stepped forward and Grandmother Leah took her by the hand and led her to the big armchair moved out into the middle of the room. A long silk train dragged on the floor with a soft and quiet rustle. The village women held their breath. The wedding gown evoked the wide world and the air of great balls of days gone by. The bride was not yet used to the puffed-up gown that rustled and murmured around her, nor to the delicate white bridal slippers on her feet, and she barely hobbled as far as the armchair.

The putting on of the wedding veil came next. Before covering her blond girlish tresses braided in village fashion, the women unloosed them so as to be able to plait separate strands. Grandmother Leah arranged with great taste and skill the light, white wedding veil and wrapped the bride's head with a wreath of artificial orange blossoms specially brought from Warsaw. The pale face of the bride was barely discernible under the veils.

The servers brought in large wooden containers of blooming oleanders trees and positioned them around the bride's chair and then lit tall wax candles in silver candelabra around her armchair.

Women relatives in their finery began gathering in the wedding room. They approached the bride, kissed her, and extended their best wishes. A number of the distinguished women guests – Grandmother Prive, Aunt Sorel, and Aunt Royze – took their places seated around the bride. The musicians set up on chairs and benches. The younger women and girls had also dressed in pink wedding garments with ribbons and artificial flowers, and they exchanged kisses with the bride.

The band played a quadrille. The girls took up positions and danced for the bride.

Chapter Fourteen

Reception for the groom. Many dozens of candles burn in silver cande-
labra. Old Hungarian wines in mud-flecked bottles. Rabbis' and rebbes'
toast R. Yoshua Kutner and the groom. The groom delivers a homily.
Sundown in summer. Grandfather's flocks return from pasture.

In the large room where the groom was sitting, everything was
ready for the groom's reception before the wedding ceremony.
Long, white-covered tables stood laden with all sorts of honey cakes
and sugar cakes and with bottles of old Hungarian wine, which
Grandfather Borukh had bought from Leybush Berliner in
Warsaw, from the well-known Leybush Lasker and other old well-
established wine merchants on Warsaw's Nalewki Street.[1] The large
and thick bottles were grimy with mould and greenish dried mud.
The bottles told of many long-gone years and of their great pedigree. Under the silver holders and candelabra, in which dozens of
stearin candles flickered festively, the wine bottles seemed to be
gaining yet more in importance and merriment. The old Hungarian wine gleamed from the bottles as part of the golden flickering
brightness of the candles and the shining silver candelabra.

The large room was full of rabbis and rebbes. Their long black
silken coats rustled and the air was filled with the strong sharp

---

1 The main street of the Jewish district in Warsaw.

smell of fur hats. The buzz of Hebrew words was heard as rabbis conversed with one another. The room was smoky from cigars and pipes. Tobacco smoke drifted in the candle light like a damp, brown mist. The candles flickered. At the head of the table, the young groom was already seated, pale from fasting. He wore a big black fur hat and a brand-new long silk coat. The several common Jews present wavered uncertainly among the rustling of rabbis. No one as yet sat down at the table. All were waiting for R. Yoshua Kutner. Uncle Yekl in his old ratty fur hat paced impatiently among the rabbis smoking a cigar.

Hirshl soon arrived, wearing his seven coats. The reek of the butcher shops of Kutno mingled with the fragrance of pipes and the smell of the stearin candles. Hirshl shouted loudly for the company to be seated at the tables because the rabbi (that is, R. Yoshua) was approaching .

And so he soon did arrive, accompanied by the rabbi of Kalisz. Those seated at the tables stood up and the people around the room made space. R. Yoshua and the rabbi of Kalisz took their places on either side of the groom.

People set to opening the old, mud-caked bottles of wine. The wonderful aromas and bouquet of the old Hungarian wine spread thickly over the tables and blended with the smell of stearin candles, pipes, and cigars. The wonderful aromas of the old wines had become nobler with time like old and fantastic landscapes or old bygone years. The wine was poured out into sparkling glasses, and it shone golden and heavy through polished glass, like the glow of a dim and dark sunset. The first one to drink was R. Yoshua after toasting the groom with '*l'chaim.*' Thereupon all drank, and noble rabbinical hands were extended and met across the table.

Then the groom began a Torah talk. He was speaking in a voice weakened by fasting. The room became quiet, and all the rabbis and rebbes listened to the groom's talk. R. Yoshua closed his eyes, glass of Hungarian wine in hand, smoking his long pipe, and smiled contentedly. He liked his beloved grandson's talk. The Kalisz rabbi, the 'Living Soul,' also listened attentively.

When the groom finished, the hands of the rabbis were once

again extended across the tables. Glasses were filled once again with dark Hungarian wines. The very glasses emitted wine fragrances as if they were hot exotic flowers. The big white stearin candles in the silver candleholders glowed in the summer evening and melted in the heat. Toasts of wine were downed.

The smells of fruit-laden trees wafted in through the open windows from the orchard. A cool wind blew from the fields of grain. One could hear the lowing of Grandfather's cows and also the bleating of sheep flocks being brought home from pasture. The heavens burnt like fire in the dark red of the sunset. Colourful clouds rested on the horizon like golden exotic ships. Frogs croaked in the little pond in the orchard. The twittering of birds was heard. People were preparing for the wedding ceremony.

Chapter Fifteen

The famous jester Noah Nashelsker is about to serenade the groom. The klezmorim play something weepy. Yontl's groom's serenade. Winds in the old Lublin cemetery. Yontl the Musician wanders over the old hilly Jewish streets of Lublin. Poplar trees rustle along the roads. The fields around Lublin smell of cedar. Peasants dance in the fields and Yontl plays a fiddle. Yom Kippur in the synagogue of Lublin. The sun is going down over the roofs of Lublin. At the time of the closing service on the Day of Atonement Yontl, standing before the cantor's desk, weeps over the hard lot of man. Noah Nashelsker preaches morals to the groom and describes what is happening above in heaven on the day of the groom's wedding. Noah Nashelsker stands on a chair and calls upon R. Yoshua to bless the groom before the canopy ceremony.

A large silver tray was set down before the groom. It bore a snow-white linen *kitl*[1] with a golden embroidered collar, also a heavy Turkish prayer shawl with a broad edging of embroidered silver lettering. The gold and silver embroidery on the background of white linen shimmered nobly amid the colours of the wines in the glasses and bottles, the candleholders and the glimmer of stearin candles on the white table cloths on the tables, and among the fruits, sweets, nuts, and cakes. All this heightened the festive air

---

1 A *kitl* is worn by the groom at his wedding, by the leader of the Passover Seder, and by male worshippers on the High Holidays.

of the room filled with long black silk coats and dark fur hats. After the groom's talk the room buzzed with voices like a beehive.

Soon it would be time to serenade the groom, and the musicians were coming in. Behind the buzz of voices of rabbis and relatives, the musicians were tuning up their instruments. Fiddlers plucked the strings of their fiddles, the trumpets and the flutes made fitful sounds as though in a bad mood. Even the little Jew with the drum once or twice banged his instrument. Soon the musicians were all set and the famous jester Noah Nashelsker, wearing an elegant well-pressed coat, climbed onto a chair. The collar of his shirt was pure white and unbuttoned and he wore a tall velvet skull-cap.

Noah Nashelsker coughed once. He looked around the long tables where the greatest rabbis and rebbes of Poland sat. He glanced at R. Yoshua Kutner, and Noah Nashelsker knew that for himself, for the old jester, this was a Day of Judgment. His reputation as a jester was at stake, and it was no small matter to sing and to speak to an audience of *tsadikim*. The famous jester, who had already serenaded hundreds of the finest Jewish grooms in Poland, now stood alone facing an attempt to succeed with his art with such a fearsome audience and he must not, Heaven forbid, stumble among the citations of the Sages that he had compiled and edited together from the Talmud and Midrashim, in order to interweave them artfully and in a seriously humorous fashion into his jester's recitations and songs. Noah Nashelsker again looked at the rabbis seated around the tables, at the burning candles, the wines sparkling in glasses, and also at the great Gaon, R. Yoshua Kutner, and at the groom. R. Yoshua was quietly waiting for the jester to begin. Noah Nashelsker gestured to the musicians standing poised with their instruments, fiddles under their necks, only waiting for a sign from the noted Noah Nashelsker.

The fiddles started playing. All together. The other instruments were still. The fiddles broke into a lament. A famous piece by Yontl the Musician from Lublin was being played, a groom's serenade, which he, Yontl, had composed for himself to perform at his own wedding. In the deep and sad outpouring of the fiddles the audience believed that they heard the original throbs of the heart of Yontl, the poor Jewish musician, on the day of his wedding. Perhaps they told of Yontl's love for his bride and perhaps about the winds among the trees in the old cemetery in Lublin, perhaps about the sombre shadows in the old synagogues of Lublin, where the hallowed dead of the cemetery of Lublin prayed after midnight, taking the awesome Torahs from the Ark of the Law and reading them. And perhaps they told of the hideous gateways to the little houses in the Jewish street in Lublin where Yontl was raised as an orphan and where he knocked around in tatters as a dreamy boy and where he became a musician at Jewish weddings. In the adagios and in the lulling rhythms of the dark melodies the listeners believed they heard Yontl the Musician wandering over the hunched and hilly Jewish streets of Lublin, stopping by night near an old wall to play his fiddle in the dark night among the little Jewish houses or even to wander, a helpless musician, in the world of chaos of the other world. At times it seemed as though the fiddles suddenly awoke from their murky melancholy depth and turned merrier. Out of the dark melodies, sunlight broke through, and the far fields and orchards around Lublin extruded their smells. The poplars rustled along the roads. In an inn, peasants drink liquor, and Yontl the Musician stands in the corner making merry with simple village Gentiles and plays joyously on his fiddle. Again the fiddles fell into deep sadness, and unmistakably, Yom Kippur in Lublin could be heard. The synagogues full of pale fasting Jews in white linen *kitl* robes and in prayer shawls. Yontl stands before the lectern reciting the closing service of the Day of Atonement, during which the merciful Gates of Heaven close. The sun goes down over the roofs of Lublin. The windows of the prayer houses are tinged with red. The dozens and dozens of nearly burnt-out long, braided candles, which stand in little sand boxes, are now just flickering gleams, and Yontl weeps over the hard lot of man and over all hopelessness.

The stearin candles blazed majestically in the silver candelabra. The orchard outside rustled quietly and the frogs croaked. The summer night was approaching fast. Stars came out in the dark summer skies. The rabbis around the tables were quiet, and the groom took out a white kerchief from his pocket and covered his eyes with it. Noah Nashelsker sensed the mood and once again made a movement with his hand as though to stop the fiddles. One by one the fiddles fell quiet, although it seemed that Yontl's tunes were still floating in the air. Noah Nashelsker first of all described the greatness of the relatives of the bride and groom and the greatness of the wedding day. In wonderful rhymes, partly jocular folksy Yiddish and part selected citations from the holy Gemara and Midrashim, he described how the eyes of all the Jews in Poland were directed towards the village Osmólsk, the second Jerusalem, no more and no less. The springs of the deepest Torah and wisdom bubble here under the trees in the orchards and in the 'court' of the Jewish landowner like the springs of the Pool of Siloam behind the Gate of Mercy of the Temple in Jerusalem. He compared the tables behind which sat the greatest *tsadikim* in Poland to the Golden Altar of incense and the candles in the chandeliers to the lights in the menorah.

From there, Noah Nashelsker shifted over to the meaning of the wedding day for the great prodigy, the groom, scion of the greatest rabbis and Hasidic rebbes. In the groom the Torah returns to its haven, and he will carry the light of the Torah and the goodness of his saintly parents deeper into the world. Imagine the wedding day of such a groom and the wedding day is compared to Yom Kippur. Here Noah Nashelsker gestured to the musicians, and the fiddles wafted up gracefully and easily from the stillness just as though Noah Nashelsker conjured them to put his ideas and sayings somewhere into other worlds. Nashelsker's leonine voice became darker and more serious amid the quiet playing of the fiddles, and he set to depicting what was going on there in the seven heavens on the wedding day of the grandson of R. Yoshua Kutner. It is just as on Yom Kippur there. All lights are lit. The good attending angels, in long white silk coats and wearing golden fur hats on their heads, have brought out the great record book of the groom's deeds, the book of his Torah and accomplishments, and the old roster of his saintly ancestors. The black dark angels lower their tails like beaten dogs and crawl into the mouse holes of heaven, for what is there for them to say and how can they open their dark devilish snouts in the face of the greatest princes of the Torah of the Jews in Poland? Therefore the dark angels lie all together in great silence and their skin crawls, but the good attending angels have opened the big parchment books. Their pages sparkle like silver snow in the blue light of the heavenly courtroom. From the great golden letters, gleaming like a thousand suns dredged up from butter casks, an angel reads out the merits of the groom and the merits of his Torah learning. The fragrance of the groom's deeds is like that of the noblest spices and herbs. Listening in are his saintly grandfathers, R. Yitskhok Vurker and R. Yoshua, and the other good men of blessed memory from whose seeds the groom has sprung. The holy departed ones expressly came from their golden chairs in the luminous Garden of Eden to hear the deeds of their grandson. And it gladdens their hearts mightily and they smile like the Divine Presence and like the suns. And the fiddles play ever more solemnly and sweetly. Yontl's melodies flow over the whole room and over the heads of the rabbis and embrace Noah's sayings like still blue waters that engulf flocks of geese, which swim and move on them. But Noah makes another gesture with his hand and the fiddles retreat and become quieter and sadder. Noah Nashelsker turns towards the groom with the following words:

'Although I am only a simple Jew and lower than the lowest blade of grass compared to the *tsadikim* sitting here, who are equal to the mightiest cedars of the forests in Lebanon, and who am I to admonish and preach morals in their presence and raise my voice in the midst of the roar of the lions? Nevertheless, even a common Jew may address a groom on his wedding day and remind him to look into his soul and reflect. Anyone may speak the truth. For is not the wedding day in its awesomeness comparable to the greatest moments in a man's life, namely, to Yom Kippur and to the day of his death?'

And when Noah Nashelsker called out passionately that the holy grandfather, the world genius Yoshua Kutner, should bless the groom before the ceremony, it seemed that Noah Nashelsker had grown taller over the chair and gotten wings. All shivered and the fiddles fell silent. It was felt in the room that a tang of the awesome heavens of the Day of Atonement seemed to have floated through the open windows and mixed with the aroma of the dark Hungarian wines in the glasses, with the smoke of cigars and pipes, with the fragrance of the cakes and fruit on the table, with the smell of the fur hats on the rabbis' heads, and with the odour of the large stearin candles which in their dozens flickered in the silver candelabra.

Chapter Sixteen

Preparations for the veiling of the bride. The older rabbis' wives unplait the girlish braids of the bride. Grandmother Khaye weeps from joy and from piety. Noah Nashelsker sets about softening the hearts of women. Colourful women relatives around the chair of the bride. Noah Nashelsker gets ready to serenade the bride in song. He speaks of the Day of Judgment. Aunt Royze weeps in her own fashion. The coarse village uncles peek through the doors. Simkhe Gayge bursts into tears after hearing Noah Nashelsker's words. Hirshl chases back the women with a red kerchief. Yoshua Kutner, the rabbis, and the groom come in to veil the bride. Hops on the head of the bride. Mazel tov. *Hirshl gestures with the red kerchief. The rabbi is coming!*

The girlish dances in the room where the bride waited had come to an end because preparations were afoot for the bride-veiling ceremony.[1] The girls withdrew to one side. Those girlish dances were the bride's parting from her girlhood. Enough of those silly light-hearted years as a girl! Now she crosses the frontier into true Jewish womanhood and places herself in the hands of the women. The older *rebetsns* shooed the girls away from around the armchair where the bride was seated. The girls felt superfluous,

---

1 *Kale-badekns* precedes the marital ceremony itself, as the groom is led to the bride to confirm her identity (an allusion to Jacob's dilemma in his first marriage to Leah in Genesis).

for the musicians had also vanished from the room. The musicians were now playing the groom's serenade. The girls hovered
among the chairs; no one paid any attention to them. They were
in fact just in the way.

The older and more skilled women set to the work on the
bride. Impatiently and gruffly and fast and, truth to tell, with a
malicious pleasure, they undid her blond village plaits. Her hair
fell over the bride's shoulders like frightened birds in a slaughterhouse. The shears about to cut them off were almost palpable.
The rabbis' wives spoke to the bride using strange Hebrew words,
which she did not understand, while they held her maidenly hair
in their hands as though it were something unworthy. The proud
Kalisz rabbi's wife gave her a thick prayer book bound in silver
covers, a gift from the groom's parents. The Kalisher *rebetsn*
leafed through the thick prayer book with her fat short fingers to
show something to the bride and scolded the rabbis' wives and
the women not to play with the silly hair but to hurry up, for soon
R. Yoshua would arrive with the groom to veil the bride.

Grandmother Khaye stood off at a distance and saw her one
and only daughter, for whom she had prayed, now in the hands
of the ill-tempered and arrogant rabbis' wives, whose chins prac-
tically trembled with great zeal and haste. The village bride was
pale and frightened and surrendered to what was being done to
her. Grandmother Khaye felt her own coarseness and how completely powerless she was against these confident foreign women.
Grandmother Khaye wept quietly, wept from fear and happiness,
and said the several Yiddish prayers for women that she knew by
heart. The short Aunt Royze, the one with the cap on her head
and with the Turkish shawl, stood on tiptoe. With great pleasure
and the spiteful joy of an old superstitious Jewish woman, she
gazed at what the hands of the rabbis' wives were doing to the
bride. For Aunt Royze it was all too little. In the midst of it all, she
exorcised an evil eye and spat in all directions, even into the large
wooden buckets with the blooming oleander trees that stood
around the bride's armchair.

In the meantime the musicians arrived and began to set up to
serenade the bride. The famous jester Nashelsker also arrived.

The bride's plaits were by then completely unbraided, unruly and untamed, and the women had stepped aside, as happy as after performing a sacred rite. Noah Nashelsker gazed at the room filled with women, ladies-in-law, and rabbis' wives. He looked at the heavy lace bonnets, at the scarves and combed-out wigs, at the colourful and black silk dresses of the in-laws, at the large golden earrings in their ears, the golden chains, strings of pearls, and at the honey-coloured amber at their throats. The in-laws looked even more colourful and picturesque, clustered in small groups around the bride's armchair and in the light of candles and lamps flickering along the walls. Noah Nashelsker looked at this colourful assemblage of women with the experience of a maestro who knows his instrument, and he knew exactly to what softness he would have to modulate his lion voice and which devices he would have to use in his patter to take full control of their feelings and evoke in them joy, hope, fear, and sadness or really unlock the wells of their tears and turn these bejewelled and bedecked women into a weeping and whimpering flock. Women's hearts are like the softest wax in the hands of a jester and he can play on them like a master on his instrument.

Noah Nashelsker took another satisfied look at the colourful groups of women. He felt how their eyes were tense with curiosity and anticipation and how they focused on his lips like bees on honey. Noah Nashelsker was still flushed from his performance in front of the greatest *tsadikim* of Poland, and he considered his present appearance a triumph and a respite. The musicians played a mournful melody and Noah Nashelsker began to serenade.

After the very first words, when Noah Nashelsker compared the day of the wedding ceremony to the Day of Judgment and spoke directly to the heart of the bride, there was quiet weeping in the big room. Through the open windows the starry summer night's fragrances drifted in. The rustling of the trees in the orchard outside could be heard in the darkness. The bride sat frightened, white as the wedding dress she wore and white as the bridal veil that enclosed her unbraided hair. Noah Nashelsker went on to paint sad vignettes of the life of man and of every day

of a person's life that could most certainly be the last day of life.
And he sensed how the women's hearts filled with dread. The
weeping became even stronger, for the other world was apparent
in Noah's words. Only the proud Kalisz rabbi's wife remained
unfazed and did not succumb to the magic of the famous jester,
but looked at him with the hauteur of a female Talmudic scholar.
Grandmother Leah's eyes filled with genteel moistness, and she
recalled her bleak orphaned childhood years after her wedding
all alone in the attic room next to the women's synagogue in
Kutno. Aunt Royze, in her cap and her Turkish shawl, who up to
now had kept silent and just looked on, all at once changed her
mind and gave out a high squeal as though she had been stabbed
with a knife.

Through the open door covertly entered the simple village
uncles wearing their silk coats and big velvet hats on their heads.
They cocked their ears and opened their mouths and drank in
Noah Nashelsker's words. The burning wolfish eyes of Uncle
Mordekhai-Ber were veiled with a moist haze while his heart
raced from great delight. Simkhe Gayge stood there too, blub-
bering loudly. Then he noticed his small frail wife, Sore Bine,
standing at the side. He fixed his red robber's eyes on her and in
a sobbing voice swore at her in a rude peasant fashion.

Noah Nashelker had started to describe the great luck of
Grandfather Borukh and Grandmother Khaye in having the
extraordinary privilege of becoming related by marriage to the
greatest *tsadikim* of Poland. The musicians played on. Soon a cry
was heard that R. Yoshua and the groom were on their way to veil
the bride.

Hirshl walked ahead, wearing all his seven coats. From him
drifted the smell of the butcher shops in Kutno. Hirshl waved a
dirty red kerchief. His one eye glared angrily. He shouted, 'The
rabbi is coming!' and with his kerchief shooed away the women
who stood in the way. The clusters of well-dressed women in vivid
colours crowded into the corners. The area around the bride's
armchair suddenly emptied except for the older wives of rabbis,
including the Kalisz rabbi's wife. From the doorway, where the
groom was waiting, a swarm of rabbis in fur caps and black silk

coats poured in. In the midst of the rabbis walked the genius Rabbi Yoshua Kutner, short, a bit stooped, with a small grey beard. The great scholarly forehead of an intellectual shone from the heavy thick fur cap he wore on his head. Rabbi Yoshua walked slowly among the rabbis, his face quietly smiled, and he kept his eyes modestly down to the floor so as not to gaze at the women. Close to him walked the groom, pale, young, and slim. The great fur hat was disproportionate on his young, noble head. The groom looked around fearfully, yet he didn't see the bride, sitting white-faced on the armchair. When they all reached the bride, the Kalisz rabbi's wife handed the arrivals a silver tray on which lay the wedding veil.

A rain of hops fell from all sides on the wedding veil on the tray, on the pale groom and on the bride. The wives of rabbis threw whole fistfuls of hops. The scared groom hastily flung the white veil on the bride's unbraided head. The music picked up. The women cried, '*Mazel tov.*' And Reb Yoshua with the bride-groom and the rabbis withdrew quickly.

Hirshl in his seven coats walked ahead of them. He waved his red kerchief and shouted in his hoarse voice: 'Away, away, the rabbi's walking!'

The women cleared the way.

Chapter Seventeen

The Havdala[1] candles burn. Approaching the canopy. Bands are playing. The Jews of Osmolin and peasants in the fragrant summer night darkness. The bride is coming. Aunt Royze carries a large Havdala candle. Hirshl sings the 'Mi Adir' hymn welcoming the wedding couple. The 'Living Soul' reads out the ketubah.[2] *The Kalisz rabbi's wife dances opposite the young couple with a traditional braided loaf of white bread in her hands.*

Dozens of long colourful candles were blazing in the raised hands of the relatives. The candles shone golden over the black fur hats. In the groom's room preparations were afoot for the canopy ceremony.

The room was crowded. The long coloured candles blazed and smoked with a sweet waxy smell. The groom wore a long white silk *kitl* with a golden embroidered collar, and on his head he wore a large, black shiny fur hat. Grandfather Moyshl and Grandfather Borukh stood on each side of the groom waiting to accompany him.

The band played an old Jewish wedding march. The suite of relatives started off.

---

1 Havdala is a ceremony marking the end of the Sabbath on Saturday night with a long, twisted, multi-wicked candle, a cup of wine, and a box of spices.
2 The *ketubah* is the Aramaic marital contract in which the groom pledges full support of his wife and promises a specified settlement in case of divorce or his death.

The mild summer night was full of the smells of the orchard. Frogs croaked in the distance. A soft breeze blew among the fruit trees. Stars twinkled in the skies. The smell of the burning candles blended with wind and night. The music floated off into the nighttime distance.

The party approached the canopy.[3] There, too, Havdala candles and torches burned. There was a buzz of people around the canopy. Out of the night – Rembrandt-fashion – fully or partly lit faces peered. Osmolin Jews and peasants, men and women, came to see the canopy ceremony. They stood, slipped deeper into the night, among the moist-dark fruit trees. The red-gold embroidered cloth of the canopy shone festively and warmly out of the night. The canopy cover was stretched out on four rods. Several elderly Jewish attendants held the poles. The candles lit up their faces and their beards. The groom's suite came near the canopy. The escorts led the groom in his white silken *kitl* robe beneath the canopy. The youngster in the white robe and black fur hat stood and held a handkerchief to his eyes. He was lit by the light of the Havdala candles and torches.

The night smelled of wind and of fruit.

Suddenly, a new burst of music was heard in the night.

The party with the bride approached from behind the fruit trees. Dozens of women in a variety of dresses and skirts were carrying long Havdala candles. Some of the older women danced a little and clapped their hands. This sounded weird in the night. Aunt Royze in her Turkish shawl walked off to one side carrying a Havdala candle as big as a Yom Kippur candle.[4] In the midst of the women with their candles slowly walked the bride, heavily veiled in white. The night wind blew gently into the bridal veils. Grandmother Khaye and Grandmother Leah led her by the hand. Behind them walked Grandmother Prive and the rabbi of Kalisz's wife. Female faces emerged in groups out of the mild summer night, fully or partly illuminated by the blazing Havdala candles.

---

3 The *khupe*, or canopy, is traditionally outdoors, under the open sky if possible.
4 Such a candle would burn about twenty-six hours.

After arriving beneath the canopy, Grandmother Leah and Grandmother Khaye escorted the white-veiled bride seven times around the groom, who continued to cover his eyes with a handkerchief. After this procession the bride stopped opposite the groom.

The attendant Hirshl sang loudly in his thick, hoarse voice the hymn 'Mi Adir.' At the very high notes, he would lift his half-blind head to the stars and nasally intone with his red, clogged nose. All seven of his coats were widely unbuttoned. In the mild summer night and amidst the rustling of the fruit trees and in the darkness lit by the Havdala candles, Hirshl's voice sounded like the wild singing of a satyr.

Next, the Kalisher rabbi began to read the marriage contract aloud. He read in a clear and measured voice. The difficult Aramaic words sounded exotic in the midst of the night's human buzz around the canopy and amid the blazing candles. Far off among the trees, peasants were firing celebratory shots. The rabbi of Kalisz continued to read clearly and calmly. He enumerated all the Babylonian jewels and garments that the groom must give the bride. Next the old Babylonian coins of the era of the gaons, in which the value of the *ketubah* consists. Then, old relics of Jewish rightlessness in the Middle Ages such as, for example, that the groom had to seek permission from the emperor to be able to marry.[5] When the rabbi of Kalisz had finished reading the old Jewish document, the Seder-Kidushin part of the ceremony began.

R. Yoshua Kutner presided as *mesader-kiddushin*.[6] The bands started playing again. Deep inside the nighttime orchard, local peasants fired celebratory gunshots. The married couple left the canopy, accompanied by the Havdala candles and torches.

By the light of the Havdala candles, the Kalisz rabbi's wife danced for the young couple with a loaf of traditional braided bread in her hands.

The night smelled of wind and fruit.

---

5 Restrictions on the right of Jews to marry at all continued in some German regions into the nineteenth century.
6 The person who is officiating at the ceremony.

Chapter Eighteen

Uncle Yekl and Yerakhmiel run out to see Reb Isaiah Prywes arriving with Shevele Prywes in a coach. The gold mines of R. Isaiah Prywes in Grzybów. Isaiah Prywes in his arrogance. Shevele Prywes, the rich man's wife. Her ten magnificent rooms in the midst of Jewish Grzybów. Isaiah Prywes and his assistants. Isaiah Prywes fights with his six sons. Isaiah Prywes wears a peaked cap with a ribbon. Prywesovkes. Isaiah Prywes fights with the shtreimel. Isaiah Prywes goes to the council by coach and wins respect from the populace. Isaiah's 'men.' Isaiah Prywes and his relatives through marriages. The Sabbath at Isaiah Prywes's. The family gathers on Saturday night after Havdala. Refreshments. Shevele Prywes in gold and jewels. Shevele Prywes and her daughters-in-law. Isaiah Prywes recites Havdala. Purim at Reb Isaiah's. Doors are open for poor Jews. Purim players. Jewish soldiers in Isaiah Prywes's salons.

On Friday, more relatives arrived for Sheva-Brokhes.[1] Every new coach created a flurry of excitement and people looked through the 'court' windows to see who had arrived. In a wide leather coach, Isaiah Prywes[2] arrived from Warsaw with his wife, Shevele.

Reb Isaiah's arrival caused a huge sensation. Everyone ran out to look. Of course, among the first spectators was Uncle Yekl,

---

1 Sheva-Brokhes (Hebrew: Sheva-Berakhot; 'Seven Blessings') is one of several festive meals in the presence of the newly-weds during the week after the wedding.

2 The surname Prywes probably derives from the Yiddish woman's name Prive (Prywa in Polish spelling).

followed by his son-in-law, Yerakhmiel. Of course, among the very first people to extend a hearty welcome to Reb Isaiah, right after he climbed down from his coach, was Uncle Yekl. After him came Yerakhmiel. Yerakhmiel was very disappointed in Reb Isaiah's coach. From the stories he had heard of Reb Isaiah's wealth, he had been certain that Reb Isaiah would probably drive up in a golden coach as kings and ministers are inclined to do. In the end, it was merely a leather coach like any other.

Out of great disappointment a shout escaped his lips: Ratse!

Isaiah Prywes was the richest man among the Hasidim in Poland. He was estimated to be worth ten million rubles. Amid the great poverty of the Jewish masses in Poland such a figure evoked truly fantastic images. Legends about Isaiah Prywes circulated among the Hasidic poor in all the small towns and in Warsaw itself. His wealth was proverbial.

Isaiah Prywes was also known as Isaiah Eisenman (Iron Man) – for two reasons. The first was that Gabriel Eisenman was his father-in-law. Isaiah had inherited from him the ironwares store that grew into the largest hardware business in Poland and became a gold mine for him. Secondly, the name Eisenman suggested his business. Isaiah Prywes's wealth grew extraordinarily rapidly. Hasidim said he had obtained a blessing from the Kotsker rebbe when he was a young man. Nothing more was needed. It meant that whatever Reb Isaiah touched turned to gold.

As was eminently clear, Isaiah Prywes never personally attained the stature he was accorded in the Jewish society of Poland. I heard much told about him. As my wife is his granddaughter, I came to know his children and the members of his household well and was able to form a picture. Like anyone whose life and good fortune elevated him higher than his spiritual values, Reb Isaiah also got his head turned as people were courteous and reverential to him because of his success alone. His head was crammed with self-delusions and he was armour-plated in complexes when he went among his fellow men, from which came much that was comic in his entire attitude.

Many tales were told about his home in Warsaw. His wife,

Shevele, was a wealthy man's daughter and had an air of wealth about her. Although Reb Isaiah lived in an apartment building that housed both rich and poor Jews, his apartment was appointed in a royal fashion. There were ten rooms full of the most tasteful and stylish furniture, valuable porcelain, and abundant gold and silver. His wife, Shevele, used to travel abroad to the most expensive spas and bring back valuable objects, French brocade fabrics, and the finest Belgian lace. Gradually, Reb Isaiah's apartment in Grzybów[3] became a patriarchal abode.

Reb Isaiah's material growth was reflected in the stylish furniture, the crystals, and the artistic gold and silver vessels, by the Jewish splendour in the midst of Jewish poverty. This Hasidic Jew's ideas about himself assumed peculiar forms. Reb Isaiah would have furnished fertile material to any psychoanalyst studying the growth and formation of both inferiority and superiority complexes, but it is beyond the scope of my memoir to delve into these things. Everyone in his surroundings treated him with veneration. In his surroundings were Hasidic paupers who eternally hoped to get something from him and waited for his kindness. No one criticized his megalomania – that is, nobody said a corrective word – and the ego of this entirely average Polish Jew waxed boundless. Although an ordinary Torah scholar, he imagined himself to be a great one. The poor authentic Talmudic scholars had to listen to his inferior Torah thoughts and novellae and even had to praise them and express delight at his erudition. Out of self-deception germinated despotism that spared no one, and everyone proclaimed Isaiah Prywes a divinely blessed authority. In his relations with his children he was more ruler than father. He implanted this trait in the character of his six sons, men like bears with all the delusions of their father. The sons had protruding stomachs and beautiful well-kept beards and impressive flocks of children, sons-in-law, and daughters-in-law. They all trembled in awe before their father. In his presence they walked on tiptoe. They led a quiet embittered war among themselves

---

3 The Jewish district in Warsaw, around Grzybowski Square.

about who should be first in his favour. This bickering among his six sons for his favour fed Reb Isaiah's self-esteem. He saw it as reflecting his chosen status and his self-esteem in his own eyes rose steadily.

In the volumes to come I shall have much to tell about Isaiah Prywes and his six sons, their households, and their ways.

To confirm his power, Reb Isaiah was forever resorting to new, outlandish ideas. Even in the traditional Jewish way of dress, a fashion regulated and fixed and thought out in every detail among Polish Jews, Reb Isaiah found opportunities to underscore his superiority. He had a leather visor with a ribbon sewn onto the standard Jewish hat. Even the velvet Sabbath hat he wore was furnished with a leather visor and a ribbon. Isaiah Prywes's hats had to be custom-made by a special hatter. His Jewish hat was different from all other Jewish hats in Poland. Isaiah Prywes's hat! The hats with ribbons were even given a special name in Warsaw, the 'Pryvesovkes,' as if there ever existed Jews interested in wearing Jewish hats with ribbons so as to resemble Isaiah Prywes, but so far no one had dared to aspire to a leather visor. Among all the pious Jews of Poland only the authentic Isaiah Prywes had this privilege. His coup respecting hats must have so spoken to his complex nature that all of a sudden he decided to fight tooth and nail against the fur shtreimel. God forbid that Jews in general should cease to wear such fur hats. Such revolutionary plans for the whole of Jewry were not one of Reb Isaiah's ambitions. He was driven by one ambition and one only: to accentuate his power everywhere. This was the power complex of an unremarkable Polish Jew whose cradle had been blessed by good fortune. And so Reb Isaiah declared war against fur hats on his own behalf and on behalf of his six sons, to wit Isaiah Prywes's sons. He never wore a fur hat on the Sabbath or holidays as did all the pious Hasidic Polish Jews but paraded everywhere in a velvet hat with a leather visor. He went so far as to wear this hat, contrary to all custom and tradition, as one of the prominent guests on the Sabbath at the Gerer rebbe's formal table, an honour accorded to him as a Gerer Hasid and as the great magnate among Hasidic Polish Jews. The older Hasidim were angered by the Reb Isaiah's brazenness at the Gerer rebbe's table, but they held their tongues. Who was there to say a word to Reb Isaiah? He was not just anybody but Reb Isaiah Prywes!

It goes without saying that Isaiah Prywes was a supervisor on the Jewish Community Council of Warsaw. Here too he demonstrated the provincial anxieties of a mediocre man. From his apartment in Grzybów to the Jewish Council it was but a few steps, but Reb Isaiah travelled there in a coach, his rationale being that it kept people from catching sight of him in a top hat, which is what supervisors wore. This rationale stressed the sacrosanct grandeur of Reb Isaiah's person.

Beyond his work with the Community Council, Reb Isaiah was a great philanthropist on his own. He did not keep close records of his business. Among his men were many Hasidic hangers-on and also many who filled their pockets in a not-very-honest way from the ample proceeds of Reb Isaiah's iron business. Reb Isaiah himself could not have had much business acumen or he would not have expended his will to power on trivialities. But who thought of acumen in those days! At that time Poland was only beginning to industrialize. Railways and factories were being constructed. However fecklessly he might have run his business and however many of his lieutenants stuffed their pockets, money kept pouring in. No figures were kept. His family was growing. Reb Isaiah affiliated himself through marriage with the richest families of Poland, though he did not regard them as his equals. He could do nothing else. He had to marry off his children. He counted his wealthy in-laws as privileged people because he had taken their daughters for daughters-in-law. He never married into the great Jewish families of Russia, who were also reputed to have millions. First of all, Reb Isaiah held Litvaks[4] in low esteem. And secondly, Reb Isaiah wished to be without peers. All were to look up to him and consider it an honour to be in his proximity.

---

4 Jews from the lands of the former Grand Duchy of Lithuania or, generally, from the east. Litvaks were generally not adherents of Hasidism or followed one of the few Lithuanian-Belorussian rebbes, Lubavitch or Stolin.

In contracting marriages he just moved his power neurosis to a
new sphere. He shed his radiance on the heads of other rich
Jewish men in Poland, who for all their wealth were no Isaiah Pryweses but only in-laws of Isaiah Prywes.

Holidays and Purim at Reb Isaiah's were famous in Poland. I
heard much told about them. The more the family grew and with
it the number of daughters-in-law and grandchildren, the more
firmly grounded became Reb Isaiah's patriarchy and his pecu-
niary dominion. His wife, Shevele, and her rich daughters-in-law
all visited the best-known watering places abroad. Valuable crystal
and gold pieces, expensive tulles, laces, and brocades accumulated, providing tangible accessories to Reb Isaiah's megalomania. He set about instituting a courtly code of etiquette in his
apartment. The burden of this etiquette, that is, the great and
rare fortune to belong to Reb Isaiah's household, was felt by his
large-bellied sons. And they did feel it with all their souls. They,
in turn, impressed the gravity of belonging to the Prywes clan on
their own families – their children, daughters-in-law, and sons-in-
law. The Prywes family became a closed camarilla right in the
middle of Polish Jewry. Its centre was Isaiah Prywes himself, in all
his ponderous patriarchy. It must be admitted: the Hasidic Polish
poor accepted this Prywes camarilla with a certain piety and a
good deal of respect.

To go up to Reb Isaiah's apartment was not a frivolous matter,
even for his six grown-up sons. Saturday evenings were reserved
for the grandchildren and for the family. Reb Isaiah would sit in
state. The big silver candlesticks, the crystal chandeliers, which
his wife, Shevele, had brought all the way from distant resorts,
blazed with dozens of stearin candles. The finest dishes were put
on the·table and expensive Tyrolean apples and other rare fruit
were served. All the other members of the patriarchal family
received their guests in their separate apartments. With Isaiah
Prywes sat his six distinguished sons and their sons-in-law and
other male family members. The windows overlooking the street
were hung with French brocades. They were Reb Isaiah's border
between himself and the dirty Jewish poverty of Grzybów. Reb
Isaiah wore a sparkling long silk coat and the velvet hat with the

leather visor. He had just recited Havdala, marking the Sabbath's close. A mould-covered bottle of old Hungarian wine still stood on the table and a splendid silver wine cup. Havdala aromas lingered around the table, smells of wine recently poured and of spices and burnt Havdala wax candles. The silver candlesticks shone on a Saturday night. Reb Isaiah smoked his usual thick, aromatic Havana cigar, seated at the head of the table in a broad mahogany armchair. Around the table, his sons along with the male members of their households sat quietly and gazed straight at Reb Isaiah with great respect and waited for him to say something.

The daughters-in-law and the female members of their households would also get together on Saturday night in the apartments of the wealthy Shevele. When going up to visit their imposing mother-in-law, they wore their very best and bedecked themselves with pearls and diamonds as for a wedding. Shevele's windows were also hung with old brocades. Crystal chandeliers and silver candelabra sparkled in the glow of the many burning stearin candles, lit after the departure of the Sabbath and the entrance of the new week. Shevele heard Reb Isaiah's Havdala and had smelled his big silver spice box, modelled like an old Gothic tower with little bells and engravings on its sides, and then returned to her rooms, where her daughters-in-law and grandchildren were gathered. Shevele herself was the daughter of wealth, possessing ample good taste, well dressed and well turned out. Her dresses were made by the best dressmakers in Warsaw, who also sewed for the wives of Polish nobility. She wore her clothes with aristocratic poise. She owned much jewellery, which she subdivided into items for everyday use and items for the Sabbath and holidays and items for celebrations and weddings. Saturday night she was still wearing her Sabbath jewellery, large strings of pearls at her throat, earrings of large emeralds set in old gold, and a big jewelled necklace on the lace-trimmed collar of her black silk dress. On top of her Jewish wig, she wore a cover woven of the finest lace. Being a small, dainty person, she looked like a little ornamental doll when sitting in her aristocratic clothes and lace and jewels in an armchair amidst her daughters-

in-law and grandchildren. Here too, in Shevele's rooms, a solemn
patriarchal mood was dominant. The women quietly drank tea in
Belgian crystal glasses, ate fruit and jams, softly chatted with each
other but never so energetically that they could not immediately
switch their full attention to the dainty Shevele in the armchair
should she have something to say.

Only once a year were the locked doors of Reb Isaiah's apartment opened to simple folk. This was on Purim. On Purim poor
Jews from all over Warsaw filled Reb Isaiah's rich rooms. Tables
were laid out with the whole gamut of Purim delicacies – holiday
cakes, meats, and fish. Reb Isaiah gave a donation to anyone who
came. During Purim his doors were open to everyone. Friends
and strangers ate and drank, enjoyed themselves, exchanged best
wishes, and even were so daring as to press Reb Isaiah's soft rich
man's hand and toast him with a *'l'chaim.'* Poor Jews wished him
success in business. Among the poor were whole troupes of
Purim players. These were the common folk, the porters and
craftsmen of Grzybów, who never had the honour to see Reb
Isaiah up close but had only been able to look up at the dark, cur-
tained windows of his apartment or listen to stories about his
wealth and about his iron chests which were reportedly full of
gold and jewels and to stories about his lordly eccentricities and
to stories about his household and about his great in-laws. Sometimes they could see a shuttered coach leaving the gates of his
house on its way to the Jewish Community on Grzybowska Street.
It was known that Reb Isaiah sat in the flesh within the coach
wearing his black top hat on his way to the Community Hall. On
Purim these poor simple Jews were costumed in rags and masks
or had paper crowns on their heads or were dressed as rebbes
with long oakum beards and sidelocks. They stood near Isaiah
Prywes and members of his household and saw his paternal rich
man's face and saw the jewels on the ears and throats of his
daughters-in-law and grandchildren, who stood in the doors and
watched the merry Purim plays. The people in costumes sang
Purim songs for Reb Isaiah or performed their plays such as 'The
Selling of Joseph' or 'Ahasverus.' Isaiah Prywes did not like the

Purim players or their skits; nor did he like common people or any singing or play-acting. On Purim, however, there was no way he could avoid accepting these poor and vulgar 'costumed' people who danced over his waxed and carpeted floors, over which stillness had reigned for years, and who now performed their colourful and merry plays on his floors. Reb Isaiah listened without animation, his face showing not the slightest reaction to the performed Purim skits or to the boisterous songs. He had no taste for them, and it was burdensome just listening to them. But what could you do? Purim! It was their day. Nevertheless, Reb Isaiah ordered that the Purim players shorten their songs and commanded that they be given money and pieces of sweet Purim loaves. He himself never touched his own warm and well-tended hands to the Purim performers' rough toil-stained hands. On the evening of Purim even Reb Isaiah's windows were for once emancipated from the heavy French brocade drapes. The windows shone richly and sumptuously in the midst of the dirty and poor Jewish Grzybów.

There were also tables at Reb Isaiah's, laid with delicacies and food for Jewish soldiers serving with the Russian army in Warsaw. Reb Isaiah negotiated with the military authorities to get passes for a hundred Jewish soldiers to come to him on Purim. Jews from Volhynia and the depth of Russia, Jews who stank of Russian birch tar, Jews who wore military caps askew on their heads, even Jews who had eaten non-kosher food from the Russian barrack cauldrons – all these sat at Purim near Isaiah Prywes, walked on his floors in their thick soldier boots, ate Purim cookies, and drank strong Bessarabian wine which never came near Reb Isaiah's lips but was purchased by him strictly for the soldiers and poor common people who ate at his Purim table. Everyone drank a most respectful toast to Reb Isaiah and all wished him success and good fortune in his businesses.

One of Reb Isaiah's in-laws was the well-known Kalisher rabbi, the 'Living Soul.' As I have already mentioned, the Kalisher rabbi was known not only for being a great scholar of the Torah but also for being a rich man, a rich rabbi so to speak. He was therefore suitable to be an in-law as well. Since the Kalisher rabbi was a son-in-law of the rabbi of Kutno, Reb Isaiah felt obliged to attend the wedding together with his wife, the heiress Shevele. He would have considered Grandfather Borukh and his family by themselves to be beneath his dignity.

Chapter Nineteen

The great lumber merchant Jacob Engelman. Engelman's court in Głaznów. Reb Jacob's 'gardens.' Guests and scholars in Głaznów. The house of study and the ritual bath. Everything is open. The sons of Reb Jacob and their teachers. R. Yoshua comes visiting for 'fresh air.' Hirshl in the lap of luxury. Everyone wishes to light R. Yoshua's pipe. Gemaras in Głaznów. Fowl and goyim in Głaznów. Reb Jacob's daughters. Between wheat and rye. Mindl, Reb Jacob's spouse, and the wealth of children of her father, Reb Leyb Kushmerak. Reb Leyb's wives and children. Reb Leyb is killed by thunder. His young widow and the faint Hasid from Warsaw. Jacob Engelman travels into his woods. The woods rustle and Reb Jacob is engrossed in a book. The Polish woods and Jacob Engelman. Reb Jacob and the landowners. Reb Jacob returns home for the Sabbath. Reb Jacob in the ritual bath. Reb Jacob eats an egg cookie and studies the Zohar. Coaches with poor Jews draw up at Reb Jacob's for the Sabbath. The beggarly horses in Głaznów. Poor women in Reb Jacob's kitchen. Everything is neglected.

Yet another of the great Jewish magnates of Poland came for the Sabbath Sheva-Brokhes and that was Jacob Engelman.

Although Jacob Engleman and Isaiah Prywes were even related by marriage, the two differed in many respects. Reb Isaiah belonged to the urban rich of Poland, whereas Reb Engelman was one of the greatest lumber merchants. Although Jacob Engelman had never conducted any business together with Grandfather Borukh, their forests bordered on one another at many points. The Jewish lumber merchants of Poland had a passion for litigation. Engelman had frequent boundary disputes with Grandfather and they sued each other for years in court. Therein was rooted their closeness – even though Grandfather Borukh . was a common Jew from a common village family, whereas Reb Jacob was the son of a rabbi and himself a great scholar with a sharp mind, and through his many sons and daughters, made marital connections to the best Jewish families in Poland and was a figure of renown.

Jacob Engelman had forests all over Poland, but his residence was the Głaznów[1] estate near Kutno. The tenor of existence in his household befitted a scholarly Jewish landowner. Jacob Engelman had scant interest in gardens or parks, flowers or fruit trees. Instead, he maintained a big house of study and a ritual bath. He hired the sharpest scholars as teachers for his many sons. There were always at Reb Jacob's Głaznów estate all sorts of Hasidic and scholarly paupers from all over Poland, 'grandchildren' of rebbes, rabbis burnt out of their homes, authors, and women's rebbes. They all ate and drank at his place. The larders were always open in the cluttered Hasidic house. Flocks of geese, hens, ducks, and turkeys that had been abandoned to God's mercy went about as virtual strays, and whoever was so inclined slaughtered and ate them. In Jacob Engelman's 'court' it seemed that market day was perpetually in progress. The study house was always full of guest strangers who boarded for weeks at Reb Jacob's, ate at his tables, soaked in his ritual bath, and studied from his books. No one asked of anyone whence they came or who they were. In Reb Jacob's household on the Głaznów estate a voice reciting the Torah was forever resounding, either emanating from strangers or from great scholarly teachers who were drilling his sons. Reb Jacob also had a number of daughters, and so at all times there were many sons-in-law supported by him in Głaznów. They too were pro-

---

1 A village fifteen kilometres west of Kutno.

vided with private teachers. Sounds of the Torah rang out from every window in Reb Jacob's residence.

In the summer, during the days of great heat, R. Yoshua Kutner was in the habit of visiting Głaznów for a few weeks. For a summer vacation, as it were. Jacob Engelman sent a coach to fetch him. It goes without saying that these days were the happiest in the life of the attendant Hirshl. When the coach stood in front of the rabbinical court in Kutno awaiting R. Yoshua, Hirshl sat for half the day on the coach box with full bottles of water in the pockets of all seven of his stinking coats. In Głaznów, at Reb Jacob's, he lived in the lap of luxury, and his duties there were sparse, consisting mostly of occasionally bringing a piece of burning pine splinter from Reb Jacob's kitchen to kindle R. Yoshua's pipe. Even that he did rarely, as there was no shortage of volunteers to light Rabbi Kutner's pipe among the guests and strangers who hung about for weeks on end. Some offered out of respect for the world-renowned genius; some out of lack of anything else to do.

Reb Jacob's sons-in-law were almost all pampered rich men's sons, with little eagerness for sitting during the long summer days with their dried-out scholarly teachers reviewing a section of the Gemara. The rich sons-in-law jumped to serve R. Yoshua in any way they could and to light his pipe. It was the best excuse for a break from old, greasy, and torn Talmuds that had been pored over by earlier students. For the volumes of the Talmud too were also open to all. You only had to ask and you could study from them and rip them. The Talmuds always bore the odour of all sorts of Jews. As for R. Yoshua himself, he, of course, rarely left the smoky room where, engrossed in the Torah, he pulled at a pipe that now and again someone came to light with a piece of burning wood. Nevertheless, every so often R. Yoshua remembered that he had come to Głaznów for fresh air and should take a little walk. Hirshl would then appear out of the inner rooms or from the kitchen, where Reb Jacob's wife, Mindl, never stopped feeding him morsels. He came clad in all his seven coats and began to officiate over R. Yoshua's walk, although he actually did nothing except carry the bottles filled with water. Hirshl passed pleasant days in Głaznów. His good eye shone brightly and his belly grew larger beneath the seven coats. Walking also with R. Yoshua were Reb Jacob's sons and sons-in-law, as well as total strangers who had for weeks been hanging about Reb Jacob's prayer house, around the food cupboards standing open in their rooms, or in the kitchen, where large and full pots were at all times boiling on the stoves.

It would be difficult to say just where R. Yoshua went for a walk. For nothing ever grew and nothing ever bloomed in the so-called orchard around Engelman's court. The trees stood with broken branches and looked like lonely cripples. People with chronic illness had snapped off their branches and used them as walking sticks. Leaves from the trees and bushes were used as toilet paper. The toilets at Reb Jacob's could not accommodate so many strangers, so people tended to their needs under all the trees. Even the Gentiles at Reb Jacob's used the trees for their humble needs. The trunks of the trees showed incisions from small knives. Boys and plain rabbinical idlers carved their initials on the trunks. On Fridays people cut pieces of wood from the fruit trees of Reb Jacob's orchard and burnt them together with finger-nail cuttings in honour of the Sabbath.[2] In the large area around and inside Reb Jacob's orchard one was conscious of the smell from Reb Jacob's ritual bath. The ritual bath was always heated and always had various people soaking and bathing in it. An additional small ritual bath had to be built for women, as the daughters and daughters-in-law of Reb Jacob could not go into the large one except perhaps very late at night.

In the above described 'fresh air,' R. Yoshua Kutner's health was fortified. There he took walks in the company of other scholars. There was a cutting exchange of fresh observations about the Torah, and R. Yoshua amazed everyone with his questions and answers. Hens, geese, ducks, and turkeys, which looked as if they were biding their time until the big day of being slaughtered and welcomed into the great pots on the boil in Reb Jacob's kitchen, ran away with a shrill clamour and flutter of wings even though,

---

2 For mystical reasons, it was considered dangerous to leave nail cuttings lying about.

as kosher fowls, they were accustomed to Jews and scholars. They were probably fleeing from the stench of the slaughterhouses of Kutno that mercilessly wafted from Hirshl's long coats. The stench no doubt smelled of the slaughterer and the poultry Angel of Death.

In the midst of this world of the Torah, Hasidism, and wanton Jewish comfort there existed another world, the world of Reb Jacob's many daughters.

True, in regard to *Yiddishkeit*,[3] Reb Jacob's daughters were above reproach. They were pious and God-fearing and walked in the ways of their father's Judaism. They married men who came from the best and wealthiest families in all of Poland and whom the greatest matchmakers in the land had proposed to Reb Jacob. The daughters never exhibited the least recalcitrance to the ways of their parents. They behaved both before and after their weddings like proper Jewish daughters and they raised their children in a spirit of pious Jewishness. Nevertheless, Reb Jacob found it fitting, probably following the example of the many cultured estates where he did business and purchased forests from all over Poland, to introduce a little aristocracy into his own 'court.' It could not be done with his sons. Sons have to be at all times under the whip of the teachers. Neglect of the Torah is a waste of this world and might indeed jeopardize his woods. Daughters, however, are exempt from the Torah.[4] Time hung heavy on the hands of girls in Głaznów, but fussing about the kitchen did not suit them. And so Reb Jacob maintained among all the teachers and scholars two or three male and female teachers to 'polish' his daughters and give them a smattering of aristocratic culture. Among those teachers in Reb Jacob's 'court' were persons who later would play a role in the maskilic world of the Enlightenment, but they did not sway Reb Jacob's daughters in that direction. They read Schiller and Mickiewicz and went for walks in the outlying fields beyond the whole Hasidic and scholarly bedlam

---

3 Yiddish for Judaism or Jewishness.
4 Traditionally, women were not taught Talmud, but would learn to read the Hebrew alphabet of prayer and of Yiddish.

around Reb Jacob's residence. There, in the fields, Reb Jacob's daughters walked amid the wheat and rye and declaimed Schiller's poems. All this lasted until their wedding days, when the girls were harnessed into the yoke of Judaism. In Reb Jacob's house there were never any tragedies. And Schiller's poems evaporated together with the girls' youth. In the rooms of Reb Jacob's daughters, flowers grew and bloomed in flowerpots, rescued from flowers left behind by all sorts of Jews who had disported themselves and caroused in Reb Jacob's orchards.

The blessed abundance of children that grew from the womb of Reb Jacob's wife, Mindl, had its roots in her family, which had huge harvests of children. Mindl's father's name was Leyb Kushmerak, one of the oldest wealthy Jews in Poland and another great lumber merchant. Reb Leyb was a virile man who had buried in his lifetime a goodly number of wives, a whole flock of them. All died in pregnancy or had simply collapsed and broken down. For although Leyb Kushmerak repeatedly married virgins and although even the wives of his later years were young virgins in the bloom of health, no woman, no matter how healthy and strong, could long bear the abundance that flowed from his loins. His children, with whom they were constantly pregnant, were themselves as strong and big and ardent as Kushmerak. After living for a number of years with Kushmerak, a wife had to make way for a younger and healthier woman. Therefore Kushmerak flooded Poland with his children. His first-born son was by some sixty years, if not more, older than his youngest. Reb Leyb's male fruitfulness really seemed to verge on immortality. A common Angel of Death would have been too abashed to approach Kushmerak's bed. He would still be living today had he not been killed by an awesome thunderbolt in the midst of one of his great forests. The great fountainhead of procreation was cut off by a natural disaster.

Let the following fact serve as evidence of the degree to which his masculine stamina infected his wives.

The last wife of Leyb Kushmerak, who alone chanced to outlive him and by a miracle emerged safely from his bed, was, to be sure, still a very young widow. Reb Leyb married her in his eighties when she was the customary young and blooming virgin. She spent some three years with Kushmerak, and after his death she was left with two living children and a baby at the breast who had Reb Leyb's energy and appetite, no evil eye intended. Nevertheless, Jewish people are not meant to live alone. Why should a young widow, even Reb Leyb's widow, be allowed to sit alone in the world with no particular reason for being alive? Matchmakers and her parents married her to a rich man from Warsaw, a Talmud scholar, a weak, sickly man with many chronic Hasidic complaints. The man was a great scholar, a faithful adherent of the Gerer rebbe, but not much of a man, poor thing. The man was unaware of how intensely the old man, Leyb Kushmerak, had infected his last wife. Leyb Kushmerak's place should not have been assumed by just any old fellow. Reb Leyb's fecundity lived on in his widow, and the new man, the fine sickly Talmudic scholar, could not keep his head above water in Leyb Kushmerak's league, and a few weeks after the wedding was moved on to the other world. I can just imagine the glance of denigration that Reb Leyb must have given him in bright Paradise.

Engelman's residence in Głaznów swarmed with people. Anybody could have the run of his poultry and his food larders and his books and his ritual bath and his fruit trees. The sound of the Torah rang out from all the windows in his house. All sorts of pious and saintly Jews lived there as if in their own father's vineyard. But Reb Engelman himself spent all week travelling through his woods or visiting the estates of Polish landowners to negotiate lumber contracts with them. It would be no exaggeration to say that perhaps half the forest rustling darkly on the Polish earth had known the clink of Engelman's axe. The oldest and tallest trees had fallen before him. The golden sun had poked its rays dozens and maybe hundreds of years ago into the now darkest and eeriest forests. And it was all in tribute to Jacob Engelman. At every opportunity, as he travelled in his coach on the lonely roads or in the trackless woods, he studied the Talmud or rabbinic law books, or he sank his teeth into texts full of hair-splitting distinctions. For he took a whole case of books with him on his travels. The woods rustled in the autumn winds, the rains poured down or snow pattered over the forest, but Reb Jacob was oblivious to the wanton voice of nature. He sat snuggled in his coach and studied while the coachman whipped the little horses. Reb Jacob interrupted his study only when he had to draw up the particulars of a purchase agreement with a nobleman. Reb Jacob's contracts with the nobles were masterpieces of legal subtlety, more abstruse than Talmudic commentary and so tangled that the best lawyers in Poland could not unravel them. Agreements with nice distinctions in which nothing was clear and simple. The brains of Gentiles couldn't make sense of them. It goes without saying that such agreements resulted in years of litigation in the courts. The courts too couldn't make head or tail of them. And so the cases went on for years. Reb Jacob's ruling passion was to hold everyone in an impasse that lulled his opponents and then to win at the end. In this way his forests were bound together with pages from the Talmud.

Most of the time Reb Jacob came home for the Sabbath. The diverse people who lived and ate at his place, some of whom Reb Jacob himself did not know, would stand in a circle around the homecoming coach and stretch out their hands from all sides to greet him. Reb Jacob was covered with dust from his travels and short of sleep and rest. His sharp mind was always active since he was continually buying forests and cutting them down and was always facing Polish landowners in court. As soon as he came inside the house and exchanged a few words with his wife, Mindl, who had a snow-white shirt waiting for him in honour of the Sabbath, Reb Jacob went to the intensely heated ritual bath, which on Friday was full of men. Reb Jacob could just manage to forge a path past the naked Jews who immersed and dipped themselves in the ritual bath. He barely found room to submerge himself among the bearded and sidelocked heads who were immersing themselves. After the bath Reb Jacob barely pulled out his smart white shirt from among the tattered and patched shirts lying on the dirty, wet bathhouse benches. The ritual bath stank exceedingly. As soon as he re-entered his house, he was offered a good helping of peppered fish and a few egg cookies by his wife, Mindl. When he had tasted thereof, for he was not much

of an eater and not much of an expert on all the good dishes that
Mindl still cooked according to the recipes of Leyb Kushmerak's
kitchen, he put on his long black silk coat and fur hat and sat
down to study the Zohar.[5]

He paid no attention to his many sons and sons-in-law in
Głaznów. They were just people hanging around there like the
other familiar and unfamiliar people, and only rarely did he see
his daughters. Reb Jacob remembered a daughter solely on the
occasion of having to arrange a betrothal for her. Reb Jacob kept
the inventory of his children on an opening page of an old
volume of the Breastplate of Judgment,[6] where they were all
inscribed with their husbands, wives, and children, as well as the
dates of their birth.

On Thursdays in the summer, wagons filled all the roads with
wandering poor people on their way to Jacob Engelman's in
Głaznów for the Sabbath. The barns and the haystacks around
Reb Jacob's 'court' were filled with Jewish beggars by sunrise on
Friday. Linen-covered wagons stood among Reb Jacob's dog carts
and carriages. The beggars' wives milled in the cowsheds and,
without asking anyone, milked the cows into their earthenware
jugs. Even the blind, gnarled horses harnessed to the beggars'
carts became cheerier in Głaznów, neighed with beggarly chutz-
pah, sprang about in the grass, or daringly limped into Reb
Jacob's stables, pushed in among Reb Jacob's horses, and ate
from their troughs. Nobody said a word. Even Reb Jacob's Gentiles made no comment. Free for all. Reb Jacob's 'court' kitchen
on Friday was full of Jewish women beggars. They took what they
fancied from the great stacks of food, which never shrank.
Hasidic Jews who entered the kitchen for coffee or tea or to light
their pipes at the burning stove could with difficulty push past the
women beggars, whose rags filled Reb Jacob's kitchen with the
smells of field and sun.

---

5 Zohar, the Book of Splendour, is a principal text of the Jewish mystical Kabbalah.
  Attributed to Rabbi Shimon bar Yohai (ca. 140 CE), the Zohar became widely known
  after Rabbi Moses de Leon of Spain 'revealed' it about 1270 CE.
6 Hoshen Mishpat is one of the major sections of the Shulhan Arukh Jewish law code.

Chapter Twenty

The Gaon of Sochaczew. His youth in Kutno. The Kotsker and Reb Avremele. The Kotsker at home. The Jewish liquor distiller. The Gentile who buys Jewish khomets.[1] *The little rabbi sells liquor not in accordance with the law. Fears of Gehenna. The distiller faces ruin. To Krośniewice. In a* bryczka *among the fields in spring. The Gaon wishes to save the Jew. The relentless law. The Kutner makes the liquor kosher for after-Passover use. The distiller feasts on geese, but the brilliant rabbis are mutually offended.*

Among the very prominent guests who arrived for the Sabbath Sheva-Brokhes was also the Sochaczewer Gaon, Reb Avremele. At the time he was still the rabbi of Krośniewice.

As a world Talmudic authority, Reb Avremele was second to R. Yoshua Kutner. He was much younger than R. Yoshua and was a son-in-law of the Kotsker rebbe. Later he himself became rebbe, together with R. Yitskhok Meir Alter.

About his youth there circulated legends like those about the youth of R. Yoshua Kutner. R. Yoshua's youth was surrounded with a folksy aura on account of his mother, the market pedlar

---

1 Liquor made from grain is considered *khomets*, forbidden leavened food that cannot be owned by a Jew during the eight days of Passover. *Khomets* in a Jew's possession during Passover must be destroyed or given away for nothing, as no benefit may be had from such forbidden food.

woman of Płock, and on account of the entire environment in which Reb Yoshua was raised. Reb Avremele's youth was passed in a purely rabbinic and saintly Hasidic atmosphere. His father was rabbi in Biała, a great man and an intense Kotsker Hasid. The boy Avremele was reputed to be a prodigy, and no other than such a misanthropic individualist as the Kotsker rebbe – he was then already among his mice and frogs – proposed to the Bialer rabbi that he take the brilliant prodigy as a son-in-law. The Kotsker rebbe had twin daughters from his second young wife, the daughter of Reb Moshe Chalfan of Warsaw, and for one of the two daughters he took the prodigy Avremele as a husband. After the wedding, Reb Avremele boarded with the Kotsker himself, and toward him the Kotsker changed much of his misanthropic behaviour. In the Kotsker's home Reb Avremele sat studying the Torah and in prayer for days and nights. The Kotsker admonished him to avoid the Hasidic idlers and do nothing more than be involved in study. In the midst of Avremele's studying, the Kotsker would even come shuffling in in his big slippers and in his torn garments and sometimes stood by the oven and listened to Avremele's Torah study.[2] It is worth recalling that between the Kotsker's room – where the floor was never swept and no window was ever opened, and where the big fat mice and the well-fed nasty frogs freely scampered and jumped about near the Kotsker and waited at his table for the crumbs that he threw them late at night – and the rest of his apartment, where his young wife reigned, there was a great abyss. In most of the Kotsker household prevailed a simple and even quite bourgeois manner of living. They ate and drank well and dressed fairly respectably. It is said that once when the Kotsker came into Avremele's room, stood by the oven, and heard the brilliant son-in-law studying aloud, the Kotsker rebbe's wife suddenly walked into the room. The Kotsker rebbe blurted out to his wife that in his opinion the oven needed to be shifted – although the oven lacked nothing.

---

2 Traditionally, Talmudic study was conducted aloud in a melody known as *gemore-nign*; so the Kotsker could listen in on his son-in-law's otherwise solitary studying.

His wife responded to the Kotsker with the following sarcastic words: 'To take care of you one needs to have a light head and a heavy wallet.' It appears that the vibrant young wife of the Kotsker, she a daughter of Reb Moshe Chalfan of Warsaw, had very little understanding of the Kotsker's individualistic, misanthropic ways. The Kotsker answered her not at all and shuffled back into his locked room, to the mice and the frogs. Nevertheless, it appears that the Kotsker loved his wife very much. During the Passover seders she sat with him at one table. In those rabbinic times and with such a misanthrope as the Kotsker, this was the greatest sign of attachment.

Once R. Avremele, in general a sickly person, fell seriously ill at the Kotkser's house. Reb Avremele suffered from lung problems all his days, and in Kotsk he developed a serious hemorrhage. Everybody thought that he was nearing his end and the future great light of the Torah that was rising so wonderfully in the young prodigy would be extinguished. Remarkably, just at the very moment that death hovered over Avremele's bed, the Kotsker exhibited a peculiar apathy to the seriously ill beloved son-in-law. When R. Avremele's condition had worsened, his father, the Bialer rabbi, went into the Kotsker to ask that he do all that he could with his prayers in order to save the great prodigy. The Bialer rabbi did not forget to remind the Kotsker of Avremele's great qualities and that he sat day and night studying. 'He stud-dies,' said the Kotsker sarcastically, mocking him. This showed the contradictory nature of the Kotsker's misanthropic individualism.

After the Kotsker's death, R. Avremele went to two Hasidic rebbes who 'led' in the wake of the Kotsker, to the Gerer Hidushei ha-Rim (R. Itskhok Meir Alter) and to R. Henekh of Aleksandrów. After R. Henekh, when the Sefat-Emet (the second Gerer rebbe) started to lead, some of the old Kotsker Hasidim split off and made R. Avremele their rebbe.

But his authority did not lie in his status as a rebbe. As a rebbe, R. Avremele did not play a large role in Poland. Therefore his fame grew as a world-class genius, and in that hierarchy he occupied a position near R. Yoshua Kutner.

These two geniuses in Poland – although the town of Krośniewice, where R. Avremele was rabbi, was located not far from Kutno – nevertheless seldom saw each other. Gaonim, rabbinic geniuses, did not like travelling and being hosted, for they were preoccupied with their books and corresponded with each other in great responsa that became famous in the entire rabbinic world.

R. Yoshua and R. Avremele highly esteemed each other, and they were so to say distant friends. For each took a leading position in the Sea of the Talmud, and they only encountered each other in great casuistic combat; by letter, of course. Once, however, a black cat ran between these two brilliant scholars. All sorts of sycophants and Hasidic plate-lickers attempted to deepen the incident into a serious quarrel, and for a substantial time there prevailed between R. Yoshua and R. Avremele a sort of interrupted relationship, although they were also sullenly interested in each other's Torah novellae.

The incident happened as a result of the following events, and at the same time it gives us a colourful picture of Jewish conditions in Poland.

In a very small town not far from Krośniewice there lived a Jewish tavern owner and distiller. He owned large warehouses of liquor, which he sold to all the taverns of neighbouring villages. Every penny he had was in his liquor. He was a common Jew, rustic, like all liquor distillers in Poland. Before Passover, the rabbi of the town would prepare a sales document for him. All of his liquor in all the warehouses was sold to an old lame Gentile. Year by year, for many years, the Gentile would listen to the rabbi reading in Hebrew the words of the sales document. Early on the morning of the day before Passover, the Gentile came to the rabbi already tipsy in honour of the fictitious Jewish sale. For the great act the rabbi put on his long silk coat and his fur hat, tied on his silk Sabbath belt, and swayed towards the Gentile as if he wanted to pray into him. In a loud voice in the Talmudic melody, he read the formula of the scholarly document. Tipsily, the Gentile nodded his head, received a few rubles, took off to the tavern, drank again, and fell asleep in the Passover mud of the town. So it went on for several years, and the village distiller felt secure that all was done as it should be.

One year, it was on the last day of Passover, the rabbi realized that he had written the sales document incorrectly. And the whole fictive sale to the lame drunken Gentile was not made as required by Jewish law. The poor small-town rabbi shivered at the thought and cold sweat poured from under his skullcap. Think of it! The rich distiller is soundly asleep in his bed dreaming no doubt of the thousands his stocks of liquor will bring him. In fact, in the course of one night the rich man had become a beggar. All because of him: a misfortunate rabbi whom the common Jew had trusted completely. Because of the faulty contract, all the hundreds of barrels of brandy were forbidden for consumption. They might not be consumed by Jews, nor sold or traded, or made even the slightest use of. Instead, the barrels ought simply to have the plugs removed and all the liquor be allowed to flow in rivulets into the town mud. Even a Gentile must not be allowed near the streams of liquor. For should such a Gentile in his happy fervour remove his cap to the unhappy merchant and thank him heartily, then the merchant would have had some benefit from the act. Oh, some satisfaction, indeed, a thank you from a drunken yokel.. But any such benefit or use of his forbidden liquor is not allowed. The pale frightened rabbi saw how the whole merciless stringency of Jewish law had landed on the head of the rich distiller, who was still unaware of the dark Job-like news. To be silent and to keep the bitter secret? Honest piety was strong among Polish Jews of the time. The mere momentary blaze of the sinful thought in his mind made the rabbi see the hell of Gehenna opening under his feet and the eternal fires burning him for millions and millions of years. The angels of destruction were licking their lips in great delight. They expect to have a sinful rabbi on their spades and to teach him a proper Gehenna lesson. The rabbi already saw how Asmodeus's[3] eyes sparkled and how Lilith[4]

---

3 In Jewish legends, a king of demons, and angel charged with operating Gehenna to punish sinners.

4 A female demon who was rejected by Adam as too self-assured and arrogant. She is reputed to seek revenge on the descendants of Eve by harming infants, especially boys before their circumcision.

fried herself in great pleasure. What a treat! A rabbi a sinner and causing many others to sin. I don't believe that the thought of not telling the truth even entered his mind. The very barrels that were in danger of being used to advantage possessed such inherent impurity that he imagined they were begging him: Pour us out in the mud, we are impure, and we don't want, Heaven forbid, to cause a world of Jews to transgress. A sinner and one who causes the public to sin, Jeroboam ben Nevat![5] Can a Jewish rabbi, Heaven forbid, be a Jeroboam ben Nevat? The rabbi's thin nostrils, the nostrils of a sickly Jew, smelled all the sulphurous tars of Gehenna.

After a sleepless night the pale rabbi shivered with dread. He was terrified of the coarse rich distiller, who was a tough Jew, quick to anger, and who knows what he might do to him. Early in the morning of the day after Passover he hurriedly put on his worn-out fur cap and his threadbare long coat, took his walking stick with an ivory knob, piously kissed the *mezuzah*,[6] sighed, and with shivering knees set out to the distiller.

The town wondered why the rabbi was out alone without an attendant in the market so early in the morning. Probably nothing; maybe trouble with the ritual bath. Things happen, some sighed.

The rabbi quietly knocked at the distiller's door. The rich man opened the door himself. He had just had his first taste of an after-Passover meal. His cheeks were red from a bowl of cabbage borsht; the fresh home-made bread and cheese tasted especially good after the hard dry matzo[7] that he had had to gnaw on for eight days in all, the poor thing. He had just taken a cup of liquor from his packed warehouses. In high good humour, the distiller

---

5 Jeroboam ben Nevat is blamed for the secession of the Northern Ten Tribes of Israel. He is one of the few figures reputed in the Talmud to be condemned to hell for all eternity, being kept in a cauldron of boiling excrement according to some accounts.
6 A small case containing a piece of parchment with scriptural verses (Deuteronomy 6: 4–9, 11: 13–21) to remind Jews of their obligation towards God, which is fixed to the frame of the doors of the house.
7 Passover bread.

waited for the carriage harnessed with two sharp black horses to take him to a neighbouring landlord. The sight of the rabbi entering his doorway seemingly out of nowhere startled him. A respectful 'welcome' stuck in his throat. He almost didn't recognize the rabbi. His face the colour of dirt, he stood trembling on the threshold. 'A tragedy, Reb Yankel.' 'What tragedy?' asked the distiller. He too felt that his heart missed a beat from a terrible premonition. 'A misfortune. Poverty, Reb Yankel, bitter poverty. You are a naked pauper.'

The dealer blinked and looked at the rabbi still standing at the door. Even the rabbi's beard and sidelocks trembled, and he just managed to hold on to his proper rabbinical walking stick. The distiller was lost. What poverty? How poverty? He thought of fire at first. But how come a fire? If there was a fire, why were the bells not ringing in town? And why would the rabbi himself run to him? 'Poverty. Not fit for use or benefit' – the rabbi shrieked in a strange voice. And still at the threshold, he explained the whole of the misfortune.

The dealer began to understand what had happened. His strong arms, used to fighting peasants or moving barrels of liquor, ached to grab the rabbi and break him up into dust and ashes. The distiller's bloodshot eyes burned with the fires of hell. The rabbi felt sure that his last hour had come. Fearful and in despair, he therefore thought that he must say the confessional Vidui.[8] Making a noise like an ox about to be slaughtered, the distiller lifted his arms, but he kept them in the air away from the rabbi's hat. First, the healthy Jew developed a sort of distaste for the doubled over, half-dead little rabbi fluttering beneath his upraised arms, eyes closed, and his beard and sidelocks glued in cold sweat and giving off an unpleasant smell. Second, he knew that without this rabbi he, the distiller, would be entirely helpless and unable to find his way at all in the deep fearsome abysses of wronged Jewish piety in which he was now involved. He regained

---

8 A Hebrew confession made on the verge of death. It is also a key part of the Yom Kippur liturgy.

control of himself with the inner strength of a common, healthy Jew and asked the rabbi:

'What is there to do?'

'We have to go to R. Avremele in Krośniewice. Only he, the Gaon, can perhaps find a way out.'

From the distiller's window was heard the sharp arrival of the proud *bryczka* carriage that was supposed to take the distiller to the wealthy landowner. The distiller grabbed up and put on his overcoat; he pulled the rabbi by the wide collar of his worn silk coat and easily dragged him along.

The two slim horses barely stood harnessed to the *bryczka*, as they strained with their heads and kicked at the ground. The distiller climbed onto the *bryczka* and with his arms almost dragged the rabbi up after him. And when the carriage gave a jerk, the distiller yelled at the driver as if he wanted to take out his great inner pain: 'To Krośniewice, to the rabbi!'

The whole way, the distiller did not say a word and sat mute. The rabbi was also silent and sat swaddled in his threadbare long silk coat. The fields smelled of post-Passover spring. The sky shone mildly. The earth was already covered with fresh grass and with the first yellow spring flowers. Young goslings and ducklings played in the thawed streams. The quiet, peaceful happiness of the awakened world depressed the mood of the distiller even more and he believed that he did not at all recognize the fields over which his carriage with the black horses had always carried him merry and happy.

In Krośniewice they went directly to R. Avremele.

R. Avremele was sitting among his books and studying aloud. He did not smoke a pipe, for R. Avremele had had weak lungs since childhood and frequently saw physicians. The distiller and the rabbi hastily yanked open R. Avremele's door and did not wait for the attendant to inquire whether R. Avremele could now be interrupted and receive them. The sickly R. Avremele was very frightened; he lifted his head from the Talmud, and seeing the anxious faces of the two Jews at the door, he rose from his rabbinic leather chair and approached the door.

The distiller's rabbi did not wait for R. Avremele to ask him anything and immediately began to describe what was involved. He spoke to R. Avremele with all the Jewish legal terms of the Halakha[9] and the entire back and forth of the difficult problem.

The distiller stood at the door in his entire massive gravity. The strange thorny Hebrew words flew from the rabbi's trembling mouth. In their exotic sharpness they were cutting into him like evil knives. There was nothing good for him in those words. Through the fault of the rabbi, he had become enmeshed in a confusion of other-worldly matters, strange and forbidding.

R. Avremele was greatly upset on hearing from the rabbi of the impending ruin of an innocent rich Jew. His expression told the distiller plainly that there was no mercy for him but only law and more law. The Gaon, R. Avremele, pulled great thick volumes from the bookshelves, books upon books, spread them on the table, looked at and turned the pages, read, pondered, searched, and then ran nervously around the room in quest of a solution but unable to find one. Then again he took more tomes from the shelves. The table was caving in under the weight of the books. He read again and ran around the room, now become a court-room.

The small-town rabbi stood at the door with his head down, afraid to look at the distiller, whose stony face was that of a man awaiting a death sentence. R. Avremele was obviously conducting a heroic battle with the Jewish laws. And it was not good. The laws would not release the unfortunate Jew; they were bound to ruin him forever.

Abruptly, the books were closed. R. Avremele sighed heavily and went up to the small-town rabbi. 'It is not good' – he groaned – 'Listen to me. Go to Kutno to R. Yoshua.' But he added with the hard sharpness of a scholar. 'If R. Yoshua says that it is kosher, tell him this and this from the Tosafot.'[10] The distiller felt that this Tosafot was the greatest and most evil of the angels of death. The other thick volumes were giving in to the power of R. Avremele

---

9 Jewish religious law.
10 'Additions,' the major Hebrew commentary on the Talmud from the twelfth and thirteenth centuries.

and were about to let the unfortunate Jew out of their clutches. Not so the stubborn Tosafot; it was relentless.

The distiller and the little rabbi hurriedly left for Kutno.

The distiller's rabbi repeated everything to R. Yoshua, and before the rabbi had finished, R. Yoshua – without looking into any book – right on the spot said, 'It's kosher.' The distiller was ready to shout with glee and fall at the Gaon's feet, but he saw his rabbi's lips moving. He knew that the evil Tosafot, his Angel of Death, would not drop the slaughterer's knife even there, in R. Yoshua's room.

The little rabbi became even paler; sweat poured down his face; he was afraid to look at the distiller. He again detected the sulphurous tars of Gehenna in his nostrils if from fear of the distiller he, Heaven forbid, would conceal from R. Yoshua what the Krośniewicer rabbi had commanded him, and with great trembling he stammered out the Tosafot.

R. Yoshua showed not the slightest emotion and remarked: 'Does the rabbi of Krośniewice think that I don't know of that Tosafot? I know of that Tosafot, but nothing. The liquor is kosher, well and truly kosher.'

Imagine what went on later, at the distiller's home: the banquets, the fat roasted geese, and the drinking in honour of the great miracle. But a black cat ran between the two most brilliant rabbis of Poland. Gossipers talked of slighting words used. Like all people who live in the realm of the spirit, Talmudic scholars are very sensitive when it comes to their dignity. The story of the liquor that R. Yoshua had declared kosher, one two three, with no great casuistic battles and without so much as looking at sources, resounded across Poland. And the relationship worsened between the two Torah centres – Kutno and Krośniewice.

Let it be said that the two brilliant rabbis were very discreet about their feelings and behaved towards each other with great respect and delicacy. They were looking for an opportunity to make peace. For a long time busybodies around them kept the fires going. At last the wedding of my parents provided the occasion, and R. Avremele demonstratively came in person to honour the wedding of R. Yoshua's grandson.

Chapter Twenty-one

Simkhe Gayge goes to the rabbis' wives. Shevele Prywes at the head of the table among the women in-laws. The diamonds in Shevele's ears. Simche Gayge loses his nerve. The Pryweses. Simkhe Gayge in the fields at night. Good Sabbath, Shevele Prywes! Simkhe Gayge cannot sleep at night. Sabbath morning in Simkhe Gayge's yard. The watering of the cattle. The rascally bullock. The ruin of the silk coat. Simkhe Gayge's great wailing.

Early Saturday morning after cockcrow, Simkhe Gayge awoke and slowly climbed out of bed. He knew that today, the Sabbath of Sheva-Brokhes (the Sabbath of the seven nuptial blessings), was the culmination of the great wedding and that the part he would play in it would top everything in his life since the time when he accompanied the others to Warsaw to buy the trousseau and was taken along everywhere by Grandmother Leah and ate the delicacies at Hekslman's restaurant. Simkhe had become attached to so many rabbis' wives that he felt he was part of a rabbinical family even though he avoided the rabbis themselves, primarily because of their rapid speech patterns and the peppery smell of their fur caps and the savage Hebrew words that stung his ears like sharp thorns. Then, too, he had not found favour in the eyes of Hirshl, who sent him away. He, on the other hand, could not endure the smell of Hirshl's coats. Simkhe Gayge made a resolution to stick to the rabbis' wives. Their consciousness of his good qualities gratified Simkhe, although it did not make life any easier for Simkhe's wife, Sore Bine. She, the poor thing, had not the slightest inkling about the *yikhes-shpilke,* the pinprick obsession with pedigree and high connections that had stung her old Simkhe. She only knew that he was irritable in her presence, stared at her with his protuberant red eyes, yelled without reason and spat out the grossest peasant curses.

Last night, Friday evening, he felt as though he were climbing up a hundred rungs of the invisible ladder to heaven. This was because of Isaiah Prywes's wife, the rich lady Shevele.

Rumours of the Jewish magnate, Isaiah Prywes of Warsaw, had already reached Simkhe in Osmolin when he knew no more than a field horse and cow, but the distance between Simkhe Gayge behind the plough or in the animal stalls and Isaiah Prywes was so great that the words travelled right past his ears. On the occasion of his going to Warsaw to buy the trousseau for the bride, he was preoccupied with Grandmother Leah, the silks in the shops, and Hekslman's restaurant. He frequently heard people talk about Isaiah Prywes in the big fabric stores, as when a seamstress boasted to Grandmother Leah that she once sewed a dress for a Prywes family member and, sitting over a large piece of roast goose alongside the Warsaw aficionados of Hekslman's delicacies, he heard strangers mention Isaiah Prywes by name. But for Simkhe, this was too a lofty a sill and the gossip too cryptic to register in his peasant spirit. The tenderness in his heart was only for his close connections with the Kutner rabbi and Grandmother Leah and the Warsaw shops on Nalewki Street and Hekslman's restaurant. His meagre imagination and narrow heart did not absorb other impressions. He had lately, during the days of the wedding, become so familiar with the rabbis' wives that the Kalisher *rebetsn,* who was so vain about her pedigrees, spoke openly with him, made use of his services, and good-heartedly called him 'Reb Simkhe.' This touched him deeply.

After the great Kiddush benediction over wine had been said by the men and the Friday night meal of Sheva-Brokhes began, Simkhe quickly left the big room of the rabbis. Running into Hirshl at the threshold, he received a few unintelligible Hebrew gibes, which clearly bristled with tones of insult and contempt.

Simkhe made a gesture with his hand and went over to the women and sat near the tables where the rabbis' wives were sitting. They were wearing their Sabbath skirts, and on their tables many Sabbath candles burned, including the new wedding-gift candlesticks with which the bride had blessed her first Sabbath candles. At first Simkhe, shrieking in his coarse voice, tried to put some liveliness into the steps of the waiters carrying long platters of tasty peppered Sabbath fish and then tried some of his 'special for women' jokes, which had always wrung a smile from a few female relatives. But he soon softened his peasant voice and the jokes fell flat. There was a new and different mood at the ladies' table.

Its cause was the rich woman Shevele, Isaiah Prywes's wife.

The fancily dressed women and in-laws chatted with one another in lower tones. Simkhe Gayge plainly saw that nobody took notice of him. Everyone's eyes were turned to the top of the table, where Shevele Prywes sat not far from the bride and between the Kaliszer *rebetsn* and Grandmother Prive.

Here too she sat like a doll. She wore a black silk dress discreetly trimmed with fine lace. Her wig was framed by a delicate lace shawl like an old Spanish *grandezza*.[1] In her ears hung and swayed two large diamond earrings like two intense points of light. The diamonds in her ears were more intense than the lights of dozens of Sabbath candles blazing in silver candlesticks on the white table-cloths. Beside the diamonds' light, there was pallor in the silver of the cutlery and candlesticks and the white of the woven table-cloths. The diamond necklace on Shevele's throat shimmered whitely and refracted the gleams of the fine black silks of her dress.

In the pleated blackness of her dress and in the brilliance of her diamonds, Shevele Prywes sat like a majestic – Rembrandt-esque – composition of light and shadow amidst the wives of the rabbis in their Sabbath skirts and modest golden jewellery.

Shevele Prywes spoke but little. She gave a quiet little smile every now and again or made a small movement with her head.

---

1 A female member of the highest class of the Spanish nobility.

The diamonds shone even more luminously whenever she nodded, just as if the diamonds themselves chose to brighten her smile. Shevele smiled in the direction of the Kalisher *rebetsn* and every spark of aristocratic superiority flared in the heart of the *rebetsn*. She wanted to show everyone her casualness with Shevele Prywes and their long-standing connection, a Warsaw connection, and how she and Shevele talked as equals.

Simkhe Gayge stood stupefied. He saw that nobody looked at him and that the Kaliszer *rebetsn* would not know him now.

He also began slowly to gaze with his ruddy peasant eyes at the small ornamental woman in silks and precious stones sitting at the head of the table among rabbis' wives in their Sabbath finery. He saw how the candlesticks shone darkly in the vicinity of the diamond flames in Shevele's ears and on her silk dress collar. He saw how Shevele barely touched her fork to the aromatic Sabbath fish on her plate. Pearls and green emeralds shone on her fingers. He saw that all the tasty wedding dishes were everyday fare for Shevele. In his ears rang anew the name Prywes, which he had heard at Hekslman's restaurant and in the fabric stores on Nalewki Street and at the dressmaker's where the bride's trousseau was prepared. For the first time it dawned on his dull peasant brain that these *rebetsns* and even the Kaliszer *rebetsn* were not the top of a tree to which he could aspire and that there were even higher and more wonderful places in the fine and sweet labyrinths of *yikhes,* aristocratic pedigree. He looked across the Sabbath candles at the small discreet woman in silks and diamonds and was as stunned as if someone had just given him a cuff on his peasant pate and roused him from a stupor. This was a Prywes!

Simkhe's first thought was to go up to Shevele and say to her, 'Good Sabbath, *Gut Shabes,* Shevele Prywes!' Yet he did not stir; his feet were as leaden as if he stood above an abyss. Courage failed him. He understood that because of this small woman nobody here knew him now. All at once he was back again in those dark times before his journey to Warsaw, back to the times when he saw no further than the iron plough and the cowsheds and the dung carts. Simkhe looked at his clumsy, toil-worn hands and at the nails behind which lay black soil from his fields. He was suddenly possessed by a sense of his peasant backwardness and the distance between himself and Shevele Prywes and by the meaning of the Kalisher *rebetsn* not knowing him today, though yesterday she had so good-naturedly called him 'Reb Simkhe.'

Like unwanted company, Simkhe Gayge roamed around the tables on the further side of Shevele Prywes. He fearfully avoided her. Nobody noticed his presence. He sat quiet and dejected. Even the waiters did not notice him.

Going home late to Osmolin, he walked alone in the night. Wet grass rustled under his boots. Trees sighed in the dark. The fields exhaled the smell of cut rye. Here and there dogs barked in the still expanse. Simkhe Gayge trod alone with heavy steps and lowered head in the summer night. In his sad thoughts he continually returned to Shevele Prywes sitting at the head of the table among the rabbis' wives. The blaze of her diamonds reduced the silver of the cutlery to a pallor, as it did the whiteness of the table linen and the light of the Sabbath candles. Absent-mindedly, Simkhe Gayge stopped walking all of a sudden and his lips suddenly spoke into the breezy summer night: *Gut Shabes*, Shevele Prywes.

In the skies the stars twinkled.

In his spacious room at home a little oil lamp burned dimly. In the huge peasant bed of many pillows covered by a coarse blanket, Sore Bine was fast asleep wearing a soiled nightcap. Her soft formless mouth was open and she snored loudly. Simkhe Gayge stopped at the bedside, and his ruddy eyes glared angrily at the sleeping woman. Hoarsely he disgorged a couple of peasant curses. Then he pulled off his boots, the silk coat, and his pants. Grumbling and angry, he lay down next to Sore Bine.

Simkhe could not close an eye all night long, and now at day-break he had left his bed early and was outside in his yard. The sun had just risen and the earth was reflecting the soft reds of morning. Birds in the trees were beginning to sing. It smelled of all the freshness of the world. From the fowlhouse came the cackling of chickens, ducks, geese, and turkeys. Simkhe let the fowl out into the yard. Hens cackled loudly and set to picking at the ground. A flock of white-and-black-speckled turkey hens majestically spread out over the yard, moving with a rocking step. The turkeys puffed up, spread their feathers, distended the red beads on their wattles, and cackled. Geese, too, scattered all over the yard noisily. Seeing Simkhe in his Sabbath silk coat, for Simkhe, still in a daze, had put on his silk coat much too early, some of the geese stretched out their necks to him and hissed.

Simkhe Gayge mechanically took two wooden pails in his hands and drew water from the well.

About to water his cattle, he unlocked the door of his cowshed. A warm smell of hay and manure hit him from the shed. The cows stood and chewed next to the troughs. They turned their necks and stared at him with their huge eyes when he entered with the water pails. He went up to the first cow and raised a pail full of cold well water to her. She breathed warmly in his face with her large nostrils and gently licked his hand. Then he brought more water for the other cows, still not noticing at all that he was wearing his black silk Hasidic coat among his animals.

He brought the last pail of water to the young bullock, which was standing tied to a trough on the side. The bullock was still an untamed little animal and playful. He loved to butt with his horns, even butting the cows' full udders, and could not be allowed to go to pasture with the whole herd. Simkhe kept him tied to the trough in the shed at all times. The bullock was afraid of nothing except Simkhe. When Simkhe patted his neck, he breathed on him with his nostrils and even licked his hand. Now at dawn on Saturday when Simkhe approached the tied-up bullock with water, the bullock turned his head towards Simkhe and jumped to the conclusion that the Simkhe in his black silken coat was quite different from the Simkhe of every other day. Even before Simkhe could put the pail near the bull's mouth, the young rascally animal enmeshed his horns in Simkhe's long Hasidic silk coat and with animalistic speed tore the whole front part.

Simkhe saw the ruin, scared to death. No more long silk coat. He would have liked to whack the bull on the head with the full pail of water, but the pail slipped out of his benumbed hands and the water emptied into the dung pile. Simkhe looked around the shed. The animals around him chewed quietly. Simkhe looked at his torn silk coat again and saw black with dismay. He knew in his bones that he would not now be able to say *Gut Shabes* to Shevele Prywes in this getup. The Jew loudly cried his heart out in the middle of his animals.

Chapter Twenty-two

Two brothers of two different fathers. The cleverness of Uncle Shimon Yosef. Uncle Shimon Yosef is good-natured, but he is quick to fight. Uncle Shimon Yosef's love for Uncle Bunem. Uncle Bunem feels deeply responsible for Jewish ways. The rich hypocritically pious Moyshe-Tevye Stanislaver. Moyshe-Tevye's struggles with the evil inclination. Moyshe-Tevye cannot, poor thing, get rid of his mighty strength. Women in Moyshe-Tevye's home. The fear of desecrating the Sabbath. The smell of Gehenna. Shatnez – the forbidden linen-wool. Clothes made of skullcap fabric. Moyshe-Tevye tans animal hides. Asmodeus and Lillith. In the reign of the wicked Lillith. Uncle Bunem with a silly Jewish woman. Beware, Bunem, you are playing with all hell! When fiddles are playing. Uncle Bunem dances 'disguised' as a 'German.' 'Such "Germans" will dance for the Messiah.'

Grandmother Leah had two brothers, Uncle Shimon Yosef and Uncle Bunem. They were stepbrothers, sons of the same mother, that is, of Grandmother Blimele. The reason was that Grandmother Blimele had had in her lifetime no fewer than three husbands, all of them great Hasidim and great rabbis. Grandmother Leah was the daughter of her first husband, Uncle Shimon Yosef from the second, and Uncle Bunem from the third.

These two brothers fully resembled their respective fathers, which meant that they had no fraternal resemblance to each other. There existed tremendous love between them and they helped each other as much as possible, yet in their appearance and in their character they were like two strangers, resembling their two respective fathers.

Uncle Shimon Yosef was a handsome broad-shouldered man with a prosperous stomach and a pair of large arms that were always restless. If they were not actually doing something, he waved them around in the air like a pair of wings. He had a large ruddy face, a long and forever runny nose, a pair of bright and laughing eyes. In addition, Uncle Shimon Yosef had a red, wild, and solid beard, which seemed to have burned around his face like flames. The beard's wilful stubble spread broadly over his face, cheeks, neck, ears, and into the running nostrils of his long nose. Uncle Shimon Yosef spoke in a thick shrieking voice, hollow as though coming out of a barrel; he seemed to talk from his gut. He spoke and laughed loudly and vividly, and at the same time kept waving his big hairy hands about.

In spite of being a devout Hasid, a grandchild of Yitskok of Vurke, and a fine Jew, he was also in many respects a man who loved nature. Everybody thought of Uncle Shimon Yosef as a tremendously handy man, and he thought of himself that way, believing that he could make everything and repair anything. Even watches. This in spite of the fact that the delicate mechanisms of the watches were so injured by Uncle Shimon Yosef's hands that no watchmaker could ever put them right again. No matter. In everybody's eyes he remained as clever as ever with his hands. Whenever something was out of order at his home, he allowed no artisan but busied himself with it and damaged it even more. But he was still known as clever with his hands. Along the same line, he was always buying bargains, and all his business consisted of hollow bargains and absurd achievements. He was always bragging that soon he was going to go to Prussia and there would buy unheard-of bargains such as no one in Poland had ever seen, and then he would sell them for their weight in gold. This notwithstanding, Uncle Shimon Yosef spent his whole life as a rather merry and very poor man and a fixer clever with his hands in the eyes of the whole family. Everybody marvelled at how it happened that such a hairy person, with a permanent cold, had

obtained such a great talent for fixing everything. In his whole
bubbly and vivacious nature, he was truly a good-natured man,
yet his fidgety hair-covered hands often blundered into Jewish
cheeks, generously delivering resounding slaps. Uncle Shimon
Yosef did this for two reasons. First, Uncle Shimon could not
abide harm being done to anybody and was always taking up a
stranger's cause. Should he see a wrong done, his fleet hands did
not hesitate, and before you knew it, the best thing to do first was
to mete out blows. Impudent Hasidim of other rabbinical camps
also got slaps. Whenever Uncle suspected that such impudent
Hasidim might talk badly about Vurke, Uncle Shimon's hands
would not hesitate long, and slaps flew about. Even in the dim
late Saturday afternoon time of the third Sabbath meal, for
instance, his hands found their way onto the cheeks of impudent
Hasidim. In an encounter with Uncle Shimon's hands, not a few
opposing impudent Hasidim came away with swollen cheeks.
Talk about being good with his hands!

On the other hand, Uncle Shimon had one big weakness and
that was for his brother, Uncle Bunem.

Uncle Bunem was the very opposite of Uncle Shimon. He was,
of course, from another father. Uncle Bunem was not tall but was
rather, so to speak, a small and frail fellow. He had a rounded
black Hasidic beard, a long pious face, and a pair of quiet Gypsy
eyes. Uncle Bunem was a peculiarly pious, laconic, humble, and
depressed man. He spent his time either praying or endlessly
sharpening his slaughtering knives and testing them against his
fingernail. From the time when he became a ritual slaughterer of
some small town, he worried incessantly that his knives might
become dull, that small defects might slip into his slaughtering,
and that he might, God forbid, cause a whole town of Jews to eat
unkosher meat, and he worried that the fingernail against which
he tested the sharpness of his knives might not be long enough.
At all times, Uncle Bunem was preoccupied with being a good
Jew; he was seldom heard to speak, walked on the side, and didn't
bother even a fly on the wall. He always appeared to have stum-
bled across an obstacle and was sad, trembling with fear of not
fulfilling his pious duty, most particularly as a slaughterer. He was

crushed by the burden of inner responsibility, and he looked on himself or on his big bloody nail or blood-covered slaughtering knives in their wooden casings with suspicion, distrusting them and himself. There was no difference between a slaughterer and a high priest in his mind, and responsibility for the soul of the Jews was an unbearable burden for a small soul like Uncle Bunem.

The terrible pious melancholy of Uncle Bunem and his incessant anxiety lest he undermine Jewish observance came from his father-in-law, Moyshe-Tevye Stanislaver. Moyshe-Tevye Stanislaver was a common Jew, not much of a Torah scholar, but a tremendously strong man, who uprooted trees and could alone take on ten Gentiles. But Moyshe-Tevye was at the same time awfully sanctimonious, terrified of the least suspicion of sin, and he saw his physical strength as a dismal imposition from the Evil Inclinations, the *Yeytser hore*. He himself grieved and worried over it. What use is such strength to a Jew and may this questioning not attract the evil eye. He was envious of the sickly Hasidim and yeshiva students who could just barely crawl, who cough and spit and are unable to lift a straw from the ground. What would he not give to be a Jew with a thousand complaints! Moyshe-Tevye therefore ate little, went to cold ritual baths for the purpose of catching a cold at least, and was continually fasting. It was of no avail. His strength grew conjointly with his fasting, the cold ritual baths served only to freshen his skin, and he became stronger and healthier from day to day. Moyshe-Tevye studied books of ethics and morality such as the Kav ha-Yashar and Sheivet-Musar, and he saw the dangerous game that the hideous Devil was conducting against a cautious Jew. Nothing helped. Gentiles continued to fear his strength, and he became more and more melancholy and pious. Truly, there were no more commandments left for him to do as specified in the Shulhan Arukh code of Jewish law. Moyshe-Tevye sought new prohibitions and commandments. Transgressions on their part chased him like nasty and bothersome flies. And for Moyshe-Tevye, a transgression was everything except for prayer, fasting, and kissing the *mezuzah*. But with it all, his un-Jewish strength ate into his marrow like a dybbuk,[1] may the merciful God save us. He conducted a bitter war with the Devil all his days.

First of all, Moyshe-Tevye Stanislaver allowed no females within sight and chased his own spouse and his own daughters away from himself so that his eyes would not alight on one. He converted his home into an orthodox Gehenna, with enormously big *mezuzahs* and wash basins all over the place so as to permit the washing of hands after any action whatsoever. It goes without saying that the darkest and most fearsome day there was the Sabbath. Here Moyshe-Tevye inflicted on his household all the fearsome injunctions in the Kav ha-Yashar and other moral tracts. Not a small thing: desecration of the Holy Sabbath! And what did not constitute Sabbath desecration to Moyshe-Tevye! He rummaged among the pots, groped in corners, yelled and tore the hair on his head, for everywhere the goblins of impiety lurked in his house. And no matter how much he tried to protect himself and struggled and wrestled with the desecration of the Holy Sabbath, it was of no help. In every nook they were lying in wait for his soul. On the Sabbath at Moyshe-Tevye's one could scarcely move a limb, walk, fasten, unfasten, or button, unbutton, cough, or sneeze. You were prohibited from making any move at all. Everything was a dismal taboo. Cold sweat covered the poor fellow as the stern and God-fearing hours of the Sabbath were approaching. For all his strength and pious stubbornness, Moyshe-Tevye felt weak, helpless, and powerless as a child. He suffered and drudged in preparation for the Sabbath, and he would rather fast a whole month or soak in the coldest ritual baths than go through such a hard job as cleaning for the Sabbath. Naturally, three stars visible in the Saturday night sky were too slight evidence for the Sabbath's end to kindle a light. The very heavens were not to be trusted when it came to Jewishness. Everywhere he suspected that the Devil was leading him to a fall in order to secure him, Moyshe-Tevye, for the eternal fires of Gehenna. The

---

1 In Jewish folklore, a human soul that wanders the earth, sometimes taking residence in a body of a living person.

skies had to be sown with stars in a big way before he, Moyshe-Tevye, would sigh heavily and with a heavy heart have a light kindled. Even then he was not entirely sure that he hadn't kindled the light in the midst of the Sabbath.

Because Moyshe-Tevye Stanislaver finally concluded that the Devil also plays his dirty tricks with clothes and he, the Devil, that is, slips *shatnez* (threads of the forbidden mixture of linen and wool) into clothes, Moyshe-Tevye's heart trembled over these concerns. A Jew orders a coat from whatever tailor and figures out whether a thread of *shatnez* is entangled in the garment. Tailors are light-hearted youngsters who do not pay much attention to whether a Jew might come to sin. And so what is one to do? Moyshe-Tevye Stanislaver cannot be expected to go around naked. For this predicament, too, his fearful brain found a way out and it was as follows. As is known, the cloth from which skull-caps are made is the very safest, most pious, and most kosher material of all fabrics, as proven by the fact that it is used for sacred clothes such as yarmulkes, fur caps, and *tallit* bags. The greatest rebbes wear and carry pious garments such as skullcaps, shtreimel fur hats, and *tallit* prayer-shawl bags. Therefore Moyshe-Tevye without undue hesitation decided: no other cloth for his clothes than the sacred and holy skullcap fabric. He had pants and coats made with skullcap cloth, in addition, of course, to skullcaps themselves, which he had made of such a size that they sat on his head like great black shining sacks and fell quite a bit over his noble forehead. In the realm of *shatnez*, Moyshe-Tevye had outwitted the Devil. This, however, was the only victory that Moyshe-Tevye had over the Devil.

As a matter of fact, Moyshe-Tevye was quite well off. It could even be said that he was rich. Because of that, and only because of that, he was in a position to offer some resistance to the dark, evil transgressions lying in wait at every step for a Jew. Moyshe-Tevye had a tannery in Stanisławów.[2] He shaved the skins of all

2 Many villages and towns in Poland are called Stanisławów. This one is a village twenty-five kilometres southeast of the town of Chełm.

sorts of carcasses and processed them in huge kettles full of oak bark. The above-named stinking kettles full of dead skins in all probability depicted for him the dreadful pictures of what happens in Gehenna to Jews who yield to transgressions. A tannery does indeed have some elements of Gehenna. Moyshe-Tevye's tannery polluted the air of half the little town of Stanisławów, and Moyshe-Tevye got under Jews' skin not only because of his religiosity but also because of his livelihood, which suggested a cross between an executioner and a Gehenna demon. When Moyshe-Tevye stood in his huge skullcap, in his pants, and in his long coat cut from pious skullcap cloth and boiled in his stinking kettles the sinful skins of dead animals, a dread must have fallen not only on others but on Moyshe-Tevye himself, and this dread further strengthened his religiosity and his fear and trembling before Gehenna. Naturally, not withstanding the fact that Moyshe-Tevye always wore velvet, the velvet was unrecognizable beneath the terrible tannery stains on it, including stains of red oak bark and of the boiled and scraped animal skins. The stinking odours of the tannery permeated his pious velvet clothes, and he carried these stinking Gehenna smells wherever he went, side by side with his melancholy fears and eternal dread of the Devil.

Into the above-mentioned very religious house, where all was down-hearted and ridden with fear and where the women went about like impurities, chased and driven away by Moyshe-Tevye, little Uncle Bunem came as a quiet young son-in-law. Uncle Bunem was a frail, darkly handsome Hasidic boy, and the hyper-religious and ascetic, masculine Moyshe-Tevye soon took him in his strong hands and frightened him day and night with the worst fears of Jewish religiosity. He filled him with disgust towards his young wife and read and retold him the gruesome stories from the Kav ha-Yashar and other moral tracts and painted the wife's bed as a horrible nest of Asmodeus and Lillith. If a Jew has to find himself there occasionally, he must know that he is going into a burning ruin only to fulfil a dangerous commandment and should guard against the smallest surplus move as he is playing – no less! – with his own life and with all the worlds. Uncle Bunem's

hair stood on end when on Friday night, poor fellow, he had to
go to his wife, who was lying in a nightcap in the horrible nest of
Asmodeus and Lillith, and there with the sinful female had to
perform the prescribed deed. With such difficult and dangerous
duties does the Torah saddle a young Jewish male! I don't know
whether Uncle Bunem even knew what his young wife's face
looked like, and he trembled around her with deathly fear.
Moyshe-Tevye's melancholia was sown into the soil of Uncle
Bunem, where it lushly grew. Uncle Bunem boarded for some
years at his father-in-law's and in great fear and trepidation sired
a goodly number of children. In the end, Moyshe-Tevye saw with
great satisfaction that Bunem was well cooled down by the cold
ritual baths and that he was good for nothing except to be a
slaughterer.

Only then were fresh terrors and weird fears heaped by
Moyshe-Tevye on the weak and ever frightened Uncle Bunem.
The rich man in his tall skullcap and stinking and stained coat
stood next to Uncle Bunem when the latter tested knives with his
long nail. Moyshe-Tevye Stanislaver trembled and tore his hair
and almost in tears implored him:

'Remember, Bunem, you are playing with eternity!'

Both Uncle Bunem's brother, Uncle Shimon Yosef, and their
mother, Grandmother Blimele, nevertheless always said that to
find such a joyful fellow like Uncle Bunem, you would have to
search the whole Jewish Diaspora.

On the face of it, it seemed a peculiar thing to say. How could
it be that Bunem the slaughterer was a merrymaker? How can
this be said of such a sickly, pale lad who shivers and trembles in
fear of Friday night when he has to – Oh, horror – perform a
commandment with a silly Jewish woman, who trembles before
his knives and for the hens and the calves that he slaughters and
that Jews eat on his responsibility, a weak young man under
whose feet the earth continually trembles and Gehenna burns?
He a master of joy?

However, it was enough to see Uncle Bunem at a wedding. The
pale, frightened face was lit by an inner joy as soon as he heard
the first playing of the fiddles. All the fearful horrors that he

carried in himself from Moyshe-Tevye's home were as though blown away by the wind. He felt better in his pious, sad soul and lighter on his feet. Uncle Bunem was famous as a dancer, and that's what he was indeed. At a wedding Uncle Bunem seems to have obtained something like wings. When the musicians started playing together in honour of the bride and the groom, Uncle Bunem forgot his slaughterer's knives, he forgot the hens that shrieked in his hands when he was about to slaughter them, and he forgot the fires of Gehenna. His black Gypsy eyes blazed, and Uncle Bunem launched into a Cossack dance so that the world shook under his feet. But Uncle Bunem did not just dance any old way; he always danced 'in disguise' as when he pretended to be a 'German.' The black Hasidic beard was tied with a red hand-kerchief, he turned the visor of his cap backwards, and then he took a colourful eiderdown, hung it on a belt, and in this way pre-tended to wear a German cape. So dressed, he danced for hours and he never tired of dancing. And the musicians were not allowed to stop playing while people wanted to dance. His brother, Uncle Shimon, and his mother, Grandmother Blimele, said that such 'Germans' will dance to welcome the Messiah and gladden the holy *tsadikim* in the great days of the future.

Chapter Twenty-three

Saturday night. The Queen Sabbath parts with the Jews. Hasidic rebbes and rabbis eat preserves, drink tea, smoke cigars and pipes. Uncle Yekl gets a cigar from Isaiah Prywes. Yerakhmiel smells the smoke. Jacob Engelman. Musicians play 'Good Week.' Noah Nashelsker sings a song of how things will look for Jews when the Messiah comes. The tsadikim *dance in a circle in honour of the bride and groom. Uncle Bunem's Cossack dance. The women, the common uncles, and the administrator Gąsiorowski. Uncle Mordekhai-Ber's feet start dancing. 'Dance, in-law!' Uncle Mordekhai-Ber dances with Uncle Bunem. Play, musicians! The* tsadikim *look on as Uncle Mordekhai-Ber, the common Jew, dances with R. Yitshok Vurker's grandson.*

After Havdala, at the conclusion of the Sabbath, when all the lights were lit, the waiters brought in fresh hot tea, aromatic preserves, and a variety of fruit for the in-laws. All the great rabbis and the very wealthy men sat at tables on which lingered crumbs from the Third Sabbath Meal, and the white tablecloths were stained with wine drunk in the sacred darkness of the Third Meal. There reigned the great satisfied calm of Saturday night. The strict, awesome Queen Sabbath had taken her leave of Jews in the glow of the benediction and to the oriental aromas of the incense boxes. Once again everyday weekly matters could be resumed by Jews and the spirit becomes lighter. R. Yoshua Kutner sat in his Sabbath fur hat at the head of the table, to the right of the groom, and inhaled on his pipe. Next to him sat the Gaon of Krośniewice, who never smoked because of weak lungs and was now enjoying his hot tea. Next to the Gaon of Krośniewice sat the Kalisz rabbi, and as behove a rich man, he smoked the big fat Havana cigar given to him by Isaiah Prywes. Next to the rabbi of Kalisz sat Isaiah Prywes in his big expensive silk coat and velvet cap with a leather visor, smoking a Havana cigar and looking benignly at the gathering. To the left of the groom sat Gershon Henekh Radzyner smoking a rabbi's pipe. Next to him Jacob Engelman, who, although a very rich man, was wearing a tattered fur hat and smoking a cheap pipe that elementary teachers use. So, too, the other rabbis and relatives smoked cigars and pipes, sipped the hot tea, and ate preserves. Uncle Jacob wore an old worn hat and a torn silk coat. He asked Isaiah Prywes to give him a cigar. Uncle Jacob smoked Isaiah Prywes's cigar with great earnestness, closed his eyes, wishing to smoke with his mind unburdened, moved his head back and forth, and his great wonder and delight made him loath to release the smoke from his mouth. Isaiah Prywes's cigar! Behind Uncle Jacob's back stood his son-in-law, Yerakhmiel. He put his nose close to Uncle Jacob's mouth to smell the smoke that Uncle Jacob refused to let past his lips. He smiled broadly with admiration and had said over and over, 'Ah … ah … ah …'

The musicians came in to play, bidding people a good week. So too did Noah Nashelsker come in alongside the musicians. Noah Nashelsker glanced at the head of the tables and he, the lion of the jesters, froze with awe. But still the jester will not be denied his song, and after the close of the 'Good Week' hymn[1] by the musicians, Noah Nashelsker sang a wonderful song of how it will be for the Jews after the coming of the Messiah. With his song he at last evoked a serene smile on the faces of the great in-laws. After the song, Noah Nashelsker felt more daring, and he called on the *tsadikim* and the wealthy men of Poland to leave their

---

1 'Gute vokh, gute vokh' is a traditional popular Yiddish hymn for Saturday night, marking the Sabbath's end.

tables and dance in honour of the Queen Sabbath, who had departed, and in honour of the married couple. There was movement at the tables and the great relatives slowly came forward. In the large, well-lit room, space was made, chairs were pushed aside, and everybody moved aside to make room. Even the playing musicians and the jester moved to a corner. The middle of the room was left for the great in-laws, who joined hands in a circle. The band played a happy tune, and the holy and distinguished in-laws slowly and heavily moved in a circle. R. Yoshua Kutner also moved together with all the *tsadikim* and magnates, and he held the groom by the right hand. The other hand of the groom was held by the Kalisher rabbi, the 'Living Soul.' The hand of the rabbi of Kalisz was held by the Krośniewice Gaon, and his hand, in turn, was held by the great magnate Isaiah Prywes. The left hand of R. Yoshua Kutner was held by R. Gershon Henekh Radzyner, and next to him Jacob Engelman skipped about happily in his tattered hat and with the cheap pipe fit for a *melamed* in his mouth. All the rabbis and in-laws were enclosed in the moving circle, and the dancing circle spread ever wider in the well-lit chamber. The band played on. In the middle of the circle jumped about and danced happily Hirshl in his seven long coats. Even his blind eye smiled. Hirshl sang loudly and hoarsely along with the music. Uncle Jacob, too, in his torn long coat and with the worn fur hat on his head, boldly jumped about in the middle of the circle of the relatives, turned his head up and down, still holding Isaiah Prywes's cigar between his lips. Uncle Shimon Yosef, with his whole width, danced in the middle of the circle. He held firmly to Hirshl's coats, stamped his feet, and waved his big fleshy hands in the air.

Only after the circle of distinguished in-laws dissolved did Uncle Bunem take the floor. He danced a 'Cossack' and danced dressed as a 'German.' The black Hasidic beard tied with a red kerchief, the visor of his velvet hat turned backwards, and a colourful 'cape' made of a featherbed stretched upwards to a belt. Uncle Bunem soared over the floor, and it seemed that the lights in the silver candelabra trembled in their flames and the mild night breezes wafted in through the windows and the earth became lighter under Uncle Bunem's feet and it too began to soar. Uncle Shimon Yosef's eyes shone with great love for his brother, and he clapped his huge hairy hands and called to the musicians to go on playing ever merrier and louder. All the great rabbis at the table, even the gaon of Kutno and the gaon of Kroś-niewice and even the glum magnate Isaiah Prywes, looked on with a loving smile on the dressed-up 'German' Uncle Bunem, a grandchild of R. Yitshok of Vurke, dancing a 'Cossack' in honour of the groom and his bride and about whom Grandmother Blimele had said that such 'Germans' will dance to welcome the Messiah.

All doors leading into the great chamber of the in-laws filled with spectators of Uncle Bunem's dance; even women pushed to look. The first to look were the common village uncles, the broth-ers-in-law of Grandfather Borukh. Although they now wore new Hasidic long silk coats and skullcaps on their heads, they never-theless kept their distance and were too shy to mix with the dis-tinguished guests. The common uncles stood beside the women in the doors and looked in. There stood old Uncle Avromke with Aunt Royze, Uncle Shimon Yosef with Aunt Toybe, and right in front stood Uncle Mordekhai-Ber with pregnant Aunt Genendl. The land steward Gąsiorowski also stood at the door with Uncle Leyzer Yosef. Gąsiorowski was wearing his old aristocratic *zhupan*[2] and held in his hand the expensive walking stick with the silver knob, a relic of his former wealth. With the other hand, he twisted his long moustache. He also smiled benevolently and tapped his stick in time with the music and in time with Uncle Bunem's dance.

The most restless of all was Uncle Mordekhai-Ber. He slid out from among the women, his eyes sparkling like a wolf's, and his feet wanted to lift him as on market days in Osmolin when he would break into a dance with the peasants and Gentile girls. He saw Uncle Bunem dance, heard the band playing ever faster and merrier, and saw how the stately and hirsute Uncle Shimon Yosef

---

2 A coat popular among Polish nobles.

clapped ever more wildly with his big hairy hands. Uncle Mordekhai-Ber could hardly stay in one place. But he did not dare join the dance under the eyes of the awesome people at the head tables, and he feared Grandfather Borukh. The long silk coat that he wore felt like a strange burden on his limbs, which were becoming ever lighter and floating.

Then Uncle Shimon Yosef noticed Uncle Mordekhai-Ber. Mordekhai-Ber could not stand still; he was being carried away. Uncle Shimon Yosef waved towards him with his huge hairy hands and suddenly yelled out to him in his deep belly voice in the midst of the music. 'In-law, why are you just standing there?' he shouted across the whole of the room. 'Come and dance, come here to dance!'

Grandfather Borukh became pale and gestured quietly towards Uncle Mordekhai-Ber to stay where he was. But the word of invitation, which had come to Mordekhai-Ber from the groom's distinguished family, from a blood uncle of the groom, fired him up and his feet started to move. He forgot his humble status and also forgot his fear of Grandfather Borukh. The music kept getting merrier and happier, and Uncle Mordekhai-Ber rubbed his hands joyfully as he was used to do on the colourful market days in Osmolin. Uncle Mordekhai-Ber set out to dance lightly, but his limbs had been turned to lead by the long silk coat. All of a sudden Uncle Mordekhai-Ber pulled off the silk Hasidic coat and quickly threw it towards pregnant Aunt Genendl. Mordekhai-Ber stood there in his trousers and braces and the velvet skullcap. His eyes sparkled and his face became red from the desire to enjoy himself. He forgot about the whole world. In his ears sounded the tones of the music, and he saw the disguised Uncle Bunem dancing swimmingly across the floor. Uncle Mordekhai-Ber began to clap loudly as his feet took off to dance towards Uncle Bunem the way the peasants dance at the annual fair in Osmolin. Uncle Shimon Yosef also clapped his hands more boldly and merrily and called again, 'Dance, my friend! Dance, in-law!' Uncle Mordekhai-Ber danced in trousers and braces. And Uncle Bunem danced towards him. Soon they stretched their hands towards each other as though calling to each other, and they held fast one to the other by the arms and danced together. The band played. The distinguished relatives, along with R. Yoshua Kutner, smoked their pipes, smiled affectionately, and looked on at how the common Jew, Uncle Mordekhai-Ber, in trousers and braces, danced with R. Yitshok Vurker's grandchild.

A year and a half later, I was born in Osmólsk in the lordly manor of Grandfather Borukh Gzhivatsh. The future rabbi of Kutno, Reb Moshe Pinkhes, circumcised me, and the world-famous Gaon of the Torah, R. Yoshua Kutner, was my *sandek*, who held me at the circumcision.

New York, 29 September 1943